JMN

W9-AXZ-067

A History of Basketball for Girls and Women

A History of Basketball for Girls and Women

From Bloomers to Big Leagues

Joanne Lannin

LERNER

SPORTS

AN IMPRINT OF LERNER PUBLISHING GROUP

To my cheering section:
Rik, Mike, Mal, and Susan

This book is available in two editions:
Library binding by LernerSports
Soft cover by First Avenue Editions
Imprints of Lerner Publishing Group
241 First Avenue North
Minneapolis, MN 55401 U.S.A.

Website address: www.lernerbooks.com

Library of Congress Cataloging-in-Publication Data

Lannin, Joanne.
    A history of basketball for girls and women:
  from bloomers to big leagues/Joanne Lannin.
      p.   cm.
    Includes bibliographical references and index.
    ISBN 0-8225-3331-6 (lib. bdg. : alk. paper)
    ISBN 0-8225-9863-9 (pbk. : alk. paper)
    1. Basketball for women—United States—History—Juvenile
  literature. 2. Basketball for girls—United States—History—
  Juvenile literature. I. Title.
  GV886.L26   2000
  796.323'082—dc21   99–050643

Manufactured in the United States of America
1 2 3 4 5 6 – JR – 05 04 03 02 01 00

Contents

INTRODUCTION

In December 1891, James Naismith invented a new game. He called it basketball. Although he invented the game for his male students, in a matter of days, women were vying for playing time on the tiny court at the YMCA in Springfield, Massachusetts. Within a month, Senda Berenson had created her own version of basketball for her women students at nearby Smith College.

Women have been playing basketball ever since. They've played in nearly empty gyms where the sounds of their shouts echoed off the walls. They've played in front of thousands of fans screaming so loud they could barely hear the ball bounce. Wherever they've played, women have moved about the court with a passion and intensity that often contradicted their place in society. For some, playing basketball was an outlet from a dreary life. For others, mastering the game inspired them to master the rest of their lives.

The women's version of Naismith's game has been a source of entertainment and controversy since the beginning. Changes in the game over the years have mirrored changes in American society. Through it all, girls and women have created a history of basketball that is rich with drama and is theirs alone.

Opposite page: Ivory Soap used this illustration in its early advertisements.

A Girls' Game from the Beginning

Soon after his arrival in Springfield, Massachusetts, James Naismith faced his first teaching assignment: Invent an indoor game that his students at the Young Men's Christian Association training school could play during the winter between baseball and football seasons.

Naismith remembered a childhood game called Duck on a Rock. The point of the game was to knock a softball-sized rock off a boulder or fence by lobbing smaller rocks at it from 20 feet away. A player needed a fair amount of skill to throw the smaller rock at just the right angle. Naismith combined that idea with another one he had conceived while playing rugby at McGill College in his native Canada. There, rugby players had broken the boredom of running the track during the winter by trying to toss a ball into a box in the middle of the gym floor. The game often ended when the players on

Opposite page: Basketball games of the 1990s only vaguely resembled those of the 1890s.

A History of Basketball for Girls and Women

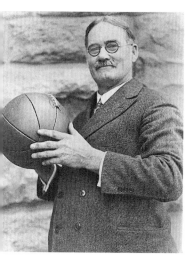

James Naismith

one team surrounded the box, making it difficult for shots to land inside of it.

Naismith decided to nail the wooden box up onto the bottom of the elevated track around the gym, about 10 feet off the ground. That way, no one could cut off access to the goal. Naismith had envisioned wooden boxes for the goals, but the YMCA's janitor, "Pop" Stebbins, offered up two old peach baskets instead. Naismith nailed up these slat-wood baskets and taught his students the game. His 13 rules included a few that have survived: no running with the ball (traveling), no pushing or shoving (fouling), and no touching or disrupting the basket while the ball is above or on the basket (goaltending). The halves were 15 minutes long with a 5-minute rest period in between.

The number of players on a team depended on the size of the court. Naismith preferred nine on a side, with three men devoted to defense, three center men, two wings, and a home man, who presumably would be the best shooter. Stebbins also had a role. He stood on a stepladder beside the hoop and retrieved the ball after it went into the basket.

Basketball remained a game for only men for less than a week. A group of women teachers from a nearby grade school passed by the YMCA on their lunch break. They peeked their heads in the doorway of the balcony when they heard shouting in the gym. They saw men passing a soccer ball from one end of the wooden gym floor to the other, intent on getting close enough to a peach basket to heave the ball with a two-handed thrust up over its rim.

Soon enough, the women were asking Naismith if they could join in. Naismith, only 30 when he invented basketball, was quick to oblige the women, perhaps because he had his eye on one of them, named Maude Sherman. He married Sherman a few years later.

Some would consider these teachers unusual women for even approaching Naismith and asking to play. Indeed, they were among the New Women of the 1890s, who had been born in the years after the first Women's Rights Convention in Seneca

Falls, New York, in 1848. More than 250 women had gathered at the Seneca Falls convention to begin the fight for equality in all areas of the law as well as the right to vote. Influenced by the efforts of Elizabeth Cady Stanton and Susan B. Anthony, the New Women of the '90s extended women's influence beyond the home into education, volunteerism, and social reform. Many of these New Women campaigned in their home states for ratification of the 19th Amendment to the U. S. Constitution, which gave women the right to vote.

In Northampton, Massachusetts, not far from Springfield, Senda Berenson, a physical education instructor at Smith College, was intrigued by the local newspaper accounts about Naismith's new game. Berenson had moved to Northampton that fall from Boston to begin her first job as a college physical education instructor. Only 23 years old, she believed in physical activity because playing sports had improved her own frail health.

Senda Berenson

Berenson was born Senda Valvrojenski in March 1868 near Vilnius, the capital of what is now Lithuania. Her father, Albert, came to America in 1874, changed his name to Berenson, and sent for his family a year later to join him in Boston's immigrant-filled West End. While Albert remained a peddler on Boston's streets all his life, he was well read and believed in education for all four of his children.

Senda's older brother, Bernard, graduated from Harvard and became an international art critic. Senda, the next oldest, enrolled at the Boston Conservatory of Music to train as a piano teacher. Because of poor health, she quit her studies in 1889 at the age of 21.

Berenson had enjoyed living on her own. She wanted to stay independent and earn a living, as her brother did. A friend suggested she enter the Boston Normal School of Gymnastics to improve her health so that she could return to the conservatory. Amy Morris Homans had founded Boston Normal in 1889. Her school trained teachers in anatomy and physiology as well as gymnastics.

A History of Basketball for Girls and Women

Berenson enrolled at Boston Normal in 1890. At first, the exercises of her daily gym classes were tiring. She thought she might have to give up and go home after all. But slowly, Berenson's health improved. She forgot about teaching piano and became as enthusiastic as Homans about the benefits of exercise. Homans selected her to fill a teaching vacancy in the physical education department at Smith College in January 1892.

As a new teacher, Berenson wanted interesting activities that would capture the imaginations of her students. When she read an item in *The Triangle*, the student newspaper in Springfield, describing Naismith's new game, she immediately set about to adapt the game for the women in her physical education classes.

Devising separate rules for women seemed like a natural thing to do. In the 1890s, reformers were touting the uniqueness of women to justify their inclusion in politics and social issues. These women wanted equal rights but not because they believed they were just like men. They believed that women had different qualities than men, qualities that made them more sensitive, for example, to the plight of the poor and more attuned to issues of morality.

Berenson embraced this philosophy in her work. She did not believe that women were suited to the same rough style of basketball that the men played. Berenson's rules divided the women's basketball court into three sections. Each player was assigned to a section and could not move beyond it. Players in the section nearest the basket were the shooters. Players on the defensive end rebounded missed shots and passed the ball to players in the middle section, who advanced the ball to the offensive end by dribbling or passing.

To discourage masculine behavior, Berenson decided that women could not snatch the ball or bat it away from an opponent. After every score, the ball returned to the center circle for a center jump. To increase the pace of what Berenson had turned into a more stationary game than the men's version, she limited players to three dribbles each and allowed them to hold the ball between passes for only three seconds. Despite these restrictions, girls loved playing basketball "with abandon and delight," as Berenson wrote in one of her journals. "No one who has seen it played can question the enthusiasm it arouses."

Physical activity was nothing new for working-class women. They were used to backbreaking work on the farm or in the factory. In their leisure time, they roller-skated, bowled, and attended dances at local dance halls. However, such pursuits were thought to be beneath middle- and upper-class women. They aspired to college for a well-rounded education that would help to make them better mothers. They were encouraged to participate—with moderation—in sedate games, such as fencing, rowing, tennis, golf, and archery, to become fit and to improve their overall health. For the most part, physical educators approved of Berenson's game.

Diagrams of basketball for women as Senda Berenson envisioned the game being played

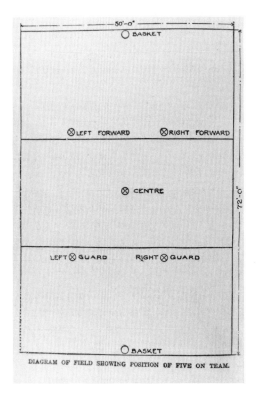

DIAGRAM OF FIELD SHOWING POSITION OF FIVE ON TEAM.

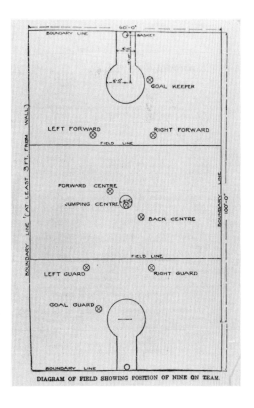

DIAGRAM OF FIELD SHOWING POSITION OF NINE ON TEAM.

A History of Basketball for Girls and Women

According to Berenson's rules, batting the ball away from an opponent was illegal.

They saw basketball as an intriguing game that fostered decision-making skills, cooperation, and endurance.

While men's teams were organizing games against other schools and local YMCAs, female physical educators decided that organized basketball games between teams from different schools created too much competitiveness in girls. Instead, they set up contests between teams of students and constantly changed the rosters of the teams.

Rivalries developed anyway. The annual spring game between the freshmen and sophomores at Smith College began in 1893. This game became one of the most popular events of the college year. One member of the class of 1895, Lydia Kendall, described the 1893 game between the freshmen and sophomores in her journal. She wrote that cheering spectators, who sang fight songs to the tune of "Way Down upon the Swanee River," filled the balconies of the gymnasium. These cheering fans hoisted the winning team's captain on their shoulders at the end of the game and paraded her around the gym.

The Boston Sunday Globe sent a reporter to cover the March 1894 contest between the freshmen and sophomore women at Smith. "NO MAN IN IT," was the banner headline, followed by a description of the 1,000 excited female spectators who decorated the balconies and frantically waved flags of violet, the sophomore class color, and yellow, the freshman class color. The sophomores won, 13–7. Afterward, fans celebrated in the streets of Northampton until suppertime.

"When a Smith girl becomes a good basket-ball player, she at once acquires athletic and social prominence in her college circles," wrote a reporter for the national magazine *Harper's Weekly* in an article about basketball at Smith. ". . . there are long days of hard exercise and faithful training and practice before the coveted honor is hers. But once the goal is reached, the reward is worth all the trouble."

By early 1894, basketball as a game for college girls was firmly rooted in the soil of New England. The winds of change were already scattering its seeds west and south.

A Girls' Game from the Beginning

The spring game between classes at Smith College became a huge social event at the college.

2

Basketball Travels West and South

Few telephones and no televisions or radios existed in the 1890s, but basketball spread quickly to colleges and prep schools across the country. YMCA instructors who had trained in New England introduced basketball to the Midwest. Naismith's former roommate in Springfield, Max Exner, taught the game to women at Carleton College in Minnesota in 1893. At Iowa State College in 1893, men and women began playing informal games on a grass court in the center of campus with net baskets suspended on upright poles. The women formed their own teams as well, with such colorful names as the Tadpoles and the Kickapoos.

South of the Mason-Dixon line, women embraced the game of basketball even before men did, thanks to Clara Gregory Baer. Baer was born during the Civil War on an island just across from the city of New Orleans. The postwar period was a difficult one for the Deep South, and educational opportunities for children were limited. Baer's father sent Clara to live with relatives in Louisville, Kentucky,

Opposite page: This team played its home games in Nome, Alaska, in 1906–07.

A History of Basketball for Girls and Women

Amelia Bloomer introduced a form of pants for women.

in the 1870s so that she could attend high school. After high school, Baer moved to Boston. In 1890, she switched her major field of study from oratory to physical education and enrolled in the Posse School, a private school started by a former Boston Normal instructor.

Baer was as enthusiastic about physical education as Berenson had been. In 1891, she turned down a job at the Boston School of Oratory to become the first instructor of physical culture at the newly opened Sophie Newcomb Memorial College, the female branch of Tulane University, in New Orleans.

Baer couldn't have picked a more challenging environment. Physical education for women was new to the South and also controversial. Many of Baer's students were driven to their classes in carriages, accompanied by the nursemaids who had cared for them since they were babies. The young women balked when Baer gave them bloomers— baggy, ankle-length pants—to wear in gym class instead of their long dresses, hats, and gloves. But after a few weeks of sweating profusely under their corsets, the women relented and changed into lighter, less restrictive blouses and leggings.

Through her Boston connections, Baer began hearing about basketball in 1892. Baer thought the game might get her reluctant students more excited about physical education. After several trials using men's rules produced objections from parents, Baer decided, as Berenson had, that Naismith's rules allowed too much roughness. She devised her own rules and introduced them to her students in early 1894. A year later, she published a pamphlet of her rules after consulting with Naismith. At his suggestion, she gave her version of the game a new name. She called it Basquette *(bahs KETT)*, a French word that would be easily understood in Louisiana where French was still widely spoken.

Baer's rules were much more restrictive than those created by Berenson. Baer divided the court into rectangles, the number and size of which depended upon how big the court was and how many girls were playing. Never were there fewer than seven divisions on her court. The divisions varied from 23 feet by 25 feet to 8 feet by 12 feet.

Baer's rules forbid any movement unless the ball was in the air. Players could not guard an opponent or attempt to block a shot. Baer also forbade yelling or talking during games. To ensure that no one girl became the star, Baer's rules called for a team's basket to be switched from one end to the other after a score, thus shifting the offensive players to defense.

As in the East, southern-style basketball called for friendly intramural games between classmates rather than contests between rival schools. But just as rivalries sprang up between classes at Smith, the annual game between the alumnae of Sophie Newcomb and a collection of the best players in the senior class became the highlight of the school year.

Baer was tireless in her efforts to enlighten everyone she could about the benefits of basquette. At the Monteagle Tennessee Summer School of Physical Culture, she taught the game to teachers from all over the South. She even staged exhibitions at social clubs in an effort to sell older women on the benefits of the game for themselves and their daughters.

One such exhibition on the night of March 13, 1895, gathered 560 female socialites at the Southern Athletic Club in New Orleans to watch the first publicly played basketball game in the South. The newspapers reported on the evening's festivities, which included a demonstration of Swedish gymnastics routines by 60 of Baer's students, followed by the main event—a game of basquette between two teams of 11 players each. The players took positions on a floor divided into 11 squares. One viewer described it as looking something like baseball with a lot of standing around in one area of the court and much activity in another. When the game was over, the players picked up the hairpins and handkerchiefs they had dropped and mingled at a reception with the socialites who had come to watch them play. Thereafter, basquette games between Baer's students and graduates of the program became highlights of the New Orleans social scene.

A History of Basketball for Girls and Women

The basketball being played by women and girls on the West Coast would have horrified Baer. It was as varied and freewheeling as life had been in the wild, wild West of the late nineteenth century. Right from the beginning, the coaches of women's and girls teams scheduled games between rival schools, feeling no qualms about fostering competitiveness. The first recorded game between two West Coast schools was on November 18, 1892, in Berkeley, California. The University of California at Berkeley lost to Miss Head's School, a girls preparatory high school, by the score of 6–5. The game was one of three played between the two schools, but there is no record of who won the other two games. The local newspaper compared the first contest to the game of football "modified to suit feminine capabilities." Each team had nine players and all nine moved about the whole court, scrambling for every loose ball and able to shoot at the basket.

Mainly women—in front of women-only audiences—played the game until the early twentieth century. *The San Francisco Chronicle,* a daily newspaper, sent a woman to cover the first game between two colleges on the West Coast on April 4, 1896, between Stanford and the University of California at Berkeley. The game, witnessed by 700 women, was won by Stanford, 2–1. Berkeley's student newspaper also covered the game.

Two weeks later, in the first recorded game in the state of Washington, the University of Washington played Ellensburg State Normal School on April 17 in Seattle. That game included one of the first recorded rules controversies. The Washington women played with an asymmetrical ball that measured $33\frac{1}{4}$ inches in one direction and 34 inches in the other. The Ellensburg women used a ball that was $32\frac{1}{4}$ inches in circumference. The referees declared the Washington ball "official" because they considered it closer to the standard size.

What was meant by "standard" is difficult to fathom since the size and quality of basketballs varied greatly in the first few years of the game. Naismith and other educators abandoned the soccer ball early on

as being too small and too hard to dribble. The first basketballs were made from four panels of cowhide, glued to heavy canvas and sewn together. A rubber bladder was inserted into a small opening and then blown up. The small opening was stitched shut with rawhide strips. The result was anything but uniform. Instruction books warned players to grip the ball the same way every time they threw it so they would get used to the shape and feel of it. Most balls only lasted a few games before they turned into odd-shaped pumpkins. By then, players had no idea which way the ball would bounce when it hit the rim or the floor. It would be another 35 years before the 30-inch ball began to be considered the true standard size.

Another controversy in the Washington-Ellensburg game ensued over what was considered

This illustration depicts the 1896 game between Stanford University and the University of California at Berkeley, which was played in a nearby armory.

A History of Basketball for Girls and Women

Women often played basketball outdoors.

appropriate defense. Both teams started nine players who kept to their own ninth of the court. But when the Ellensburg players had the ball, the Washington players tried to bat it out of their hands. Ellensburg's rules didn't allow this. Again, the Washington rules prevailed, even though the Ellensburg coach argued that the no-batting or snatching rules were better suited to women than the Washington rules. Not surprisingly, Washington won the contest, 6–3.

Washington's prowess not withstanding, Berkeley was still the team to beat on the West Coast by 1898. Berkeley was easily defeating the other colleges, high schools, private schools, and YWCA teams it played on a regular basis in the Bay Area. For instance, Berkeley defeated Mills College 13–1 and the Mission YWCA by a score of 10–1 early in 1898. For a challenge, the team scheduled a game with the

University of Nevada at Reno, to be played on April 9, 1898. The Reno players were treated to lunch at one of the dorms on campus and stayed at the homes of the players that night.

The next day, Berkeley continued its dominance in basketball, winning 14–1. *The San Francisco Chronicle* article praised Berkeley for having as many tricks and as much guile as the Stanford football team. One trick was to lure the Nevada players into a group and then suddenly roll the ball between their legs to a player on the other side of the bunch who would have an easy shot at the hoop. Despite the lopsided score, the Nevada team had enjoyed the trip so much that another one was scheduled for the 1899 season.

Nevada practiced hard for the rematch, to be played at the Odd-Fellows Hall in San Francisco on April 8, 1899. Their new coach, Ada Edwards, had been an assistant at Stanford. She taught the girls to play more aggressively and to go after every loose ball. Consequently, this game was rougher than the game the year before had been. One Nevada girl broke her nose when she was elbowed during a scramble for the ball. Berkeley won again, 7–3, but the game was much more exciting for the all-female crowd to watch.

Men were not completely excluded from watching women play basketball in those early days. If a game was played outdoors, as some high school and college games were, men were allowed to witness the action. Enterprising young men found a way to watch some indoor games as well. In 1899, the San Francisco newspaper wrote about eight high school boys who watched the entire Berkeley–Stockton High game disguised in dresses, heavy veils, gloves, and stockings.

Basketball spread more slowly to the southern part of California, where the first recorded game was an exhibition staged at the end of the 1897 Southern California Lawn Tennis Association's annual tournament in Santa Monica. This game was played between three male tennis players and seven women tennis players before an all-female crowd.

A History of
Basketball for Girls
and Women

One of the women was Marion Jones, the best female tennis player of her day, who went on to win a bronze medal in tennis at the 1900 Olympic Games in Paris.

The local newspaper described the exhibition game as a wild contest that featured the women clutching, grabbing, and pulling the hair of their male opponents in an effort to get at the ball. Unlike the women in Clara Baer's New Orleans classes, the tennis players shouted to each other as they played, roaming the whole court in pursuit of the ball. No mention was made of the outcome, but the newspaper said the men were so winded they needed to use a pair of bellows to regain their breath. The men also "shed so much perspiration that the lawn is forever protected against drought."

Private schools led the way in introducing basketball to the girls and women of Southern California in the late 1890s. Pasadena had three schools with organized basketball teams that played each other regularly and drew lots of attention. One of the local orange growers associations put a Pomona College female basketball player on the label that adorned its orange crates.

By the turn of the century, Southern California basketball had evolved into an indoor or outdoor court divided into three sections. As elsewhere, the players stayed in their respective divisions and could not dribble or run with the ball. Most early games were played with nine players on a side.

Pasadena High School became an early powerhouse in girls basketball because of a trio of sisters: Violet, Florence, and May Sutton. Pasadena teams played with only five players on the court at a time. In such games, the Sutton sisters were the whole offense, with May and Florence at forward and Violet at center.

The youngest sister, May, went on to become the first American woman to win the Wimbledon singles tennis championship, in 1905. She teamed with Marion Jones, the woman who had played in Southern California's first coed basketball exhibition game in 1897, to win the Wimbledon doubles tournament in 1903. During the school year, though, May's passion was basketball. As a 12-year-old in 1900, she was the youngest starter on Pasadena High's undefeated basketball team, which rolled over its competition, usually by such lopsided scores as 25-2. In one 1901 game, May scored 13 of the team's 15 points.

In 1903, 33 girls tried out for the Pasadena High team. Florence and Violet had graduated, but May still anchored the offense at right forward. Pasadena had a new league to compete in by then. Eight high schools, private schools, and colleges joined to form the Girls Basketball League of Southern California—the first organized league on the West Coast. Pasadena once again dominated the scene and took the season championship. It won a game against Los Angeles High by the lopsided score of 95-0 and defeated the only team that had beaten it in 1902, Marlborough High, by a score of 25-15.

Basketball's popularity in Southern California spread to grammar schools, colleges, and play-grounds, but few men played the game in the early 1900s. There is no mention in any major newspaper of a boys school team or a men's college team play-ing basketball on the West Coast until 1907.

Basketball was not for sissies or the faint of heart. Complaints were growing that the game had become too rough and freewheeling. *The Los Angeles Times* described a game between Long Beach and Los Angeles high schools in the early 1900s this way: "There was something disquieting in the grim and murderous determination with which young ladies chased each other over the court."

As concerns and complaints grew nationwide right along with the game's popularity, physical edu-cators everywhere grappled with an ironic question: How to tame girls basketball?

"There was something disquieting in the grim and murderous determination with which young ladies chased each other over the court."

3

CHANGING THE RULES

By the turn of the century, Senda Berenson was a well-respected college professor who earned $1,200 a year. She had recruited three other Boston Normal graduates, including her younger sister Bessie, to join the Smith College physical education department. The women at Smith and other colleges were playing other rigorous sports, such as field hockey, but basketball was by far the most popular.

Berenson and a group of physical educators formed a committee to address the growing concerns over basketball's roughness, as well as complaints about the many versions of the game. Committee members included Luther Gulick Jr., who had urged Naismith to invent the game in 1891, and Alice Bertha Foster, a physical education professor at Bryn Mawr College outside of Philadelphia.

In 1901, the committee published its first set of rules for women's basketball. Those first rules closely followed Berenson's original design. The court was divided into three equal parts. Snatching or batting the ball was not permitted. Holding the ball for more than three seconds was a foul. Players could only bounce the ball three times before a pass or a shot. Teams consisted of 5 to 10 players, depending on the size of the court.

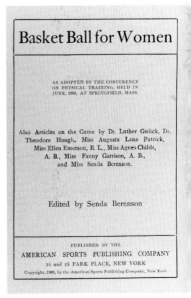

Opposite page: Senda Berenson is about to toss the ball to start a game. Above: Berenson helped write the first rulebook for women's basketball.

27

*Field hockey was
another popular sport
for young women.*

Many teams adopted the new rules, but many others ignored them. Men who were coaching women's teams preferred the men's rules and continued to use them with their women's teams, especially in the western part of the country and in states such as Texas and Kentucky. At least, the committee members decided, if two teams that used different rules were playing each other, they had a standard set on which to compromise.

The rule changes and standardization did little to quell the fears, especially on the East Coast, about girls playing basketball. Critics still considered basketball too rough and taxing a sport for women. They said that women's physical differences made them more susceptible to injury and disease. Some doctors believed that running strained women's smaller hearts. Many doctors cautioned against allowing girls to play during the first three days of menstruation. Foster only allowed her Bryn Mawr girls to play basketball if they were already well conditioned from other sports, such as field hockey. Even Berenson feared that basketball was becoming too physical. She warned that parents and school administrators would ban basketball if something were not done to preserve the sport's genteel nature.

"Unless a game as exciting as basketball is carefully guided by such rules as will eliminate roughness, the great desire to win and the excitement of the game will make our women do sadly, unwomanly things," Berenson wrote in the first basketball guide, published in 1901. "A certain amount of roughness is deemed necessary to bring out manliness in our young men. Surely, rough play can have no possible excuse in our young women."

Despite these concerns, basketball grew in popularity in the early 1900s, especially at high schools and among working-class girls. New York City and surrounding towns had an organized high school basketball league by 1900 that played in front of big crowds at local armories. In Iowa, church basements were the sites of the earliest girls basketball games. Players could bank the ball off the wall in a billiards-like variation of the bounce pass.

In many cities and towns across the states, college women home on vacation taught the game to local girls. Many girls in Westbrook, Maine, learned to play basketball because of Lois Warren, the daughter of the S. D. Warren paper mill's manager, John Warren. Lois Warren came home from Vassar College in the summer of 1902 and organized two teams of mill girls for games on the backyard court at her family home across the street from the mill. The girls from the paper sorting room were called the Crimsons and girls who sorted rags were called the Blues.

"We played mostly on grassy ground at a spot in the back of the house," recalled Susie Gilman, one of the paper sorters, in 1953. "Although those bloomers contained yards of cloth, our mothers thought them immodest and we wore our skirts over them, to and from games."

By the following winter, high school girls all over southern Maine were playing basketball. *The Portland Evening Express* in Portland, Maine, described the big crowd that came up from Saco, 20 miles away, to watch their high school girls, in their "natty, dark gray suits and red sashes," play Westbrook in February 1903. A reception for players and fans followed the game, which Westbrook won, 35–7. In another game that winter, the Gould Academy girls traveled west from Fryeburg, 50 miles away, to play the girls from Westbrook. *The Portland Evening Express* reported on the many fouls

Outdoor basketball was most often played on grass courts and in front of women spectators.

*Lucille Eaton
Hill called the
excitement of
the game an
"evil influence
upon the
emotional and
nervous
feminine
nature."*

in the low-scoring game, which Westbrook won, 12–7. The writer attributed the fouls to the fact that Gould Academy was accustomed to playing by boys rules.

But pressure continued to mount against girls playing basketball, especially at the college level. Lucille Eaton Hill of Wellesley College in Massachusetts spoke out in 1903 at a meeting of the New England Association of Colleges and Preparatory Schools. Hill warned that basketball could do permanent harm to young girls' beauty and health at a critical time in their development. She called the excitement of the game an "evil influence upon the emotional and nervous feminine nature." And she worried that basketball would "unsex" the females who played it.

In 1903, the committee tried to tame the game somewhat by adopting a new out-of-bounds rule that awarded the ball to the opponent of the player who caused it to go out. Before that, players scrambled after the ball when it went out of bounds, sometimes chasing it down stairwells and into the hallways beyond the gym in a free-for-all of pushing, shoving, screaming, shouting, and falling. Some schools had erected chicken wire fences around their basketball courts to eliminate the long-distance chases after a ball. That's why basketball players— men especially—were known as cagers before the turn of the century.

In 1903, rulemakers also changed the number of players allowed on each team. Instead of 5 to 10, the number was changed to 6 to 9. Five seemed to put too much pressure on the center who played alone in the middle court. And 10 seemed to be too many— often leading to collisions and pileups under the baskets. Courts varied greatly in those days, as the game often was played outside in open fields as well as inside cramped little gyms. Committee members who worried about women getting worn out on a big court advocated leaving some flexibility in the rules. Strangely, the one rule change that would have alleviated the fears of fatigue—allowing substitutions— was not considered.

Given all the interruptions in a typical game, it's hard to imagine why anyone worried about women collapsing from exhaustion. In 1903, many schools still used baskets with bottoms in them for the goal. After each score, play was stopped so that the ball could be retrieved out of the basket either by poking it up through the top with a long stick or by pulling a chain attached to a pulley that tipped the basket and allowed the ball to tumble out. Even after the Narraganset Machine Company began distributing its iron-rimmed hoop with braided cord netting, it was against the rules to leave the bottom of the nets open. Officials feared that the ball would fall through the cords so quickly that it might be difficult to tell if a basket had been scored.

Play also stopped for foul shots. In the early 1900s, many infractions warranted a foul shot. Such things as holding the ball for more than three seconds, stepping on the out-of-bounds line, and double-teaming a player attempting to take a shot constituted fouls.

The critics still complained loudly that basketball brought out the worst aspects of competitiveness in young women. Newspaper stories that described girls wanting to use an opponent's "neck for a stepladder" or relating how one Irish lass, emulating her ancestors, "swung right and left like the mighty Brian Boru of old," didn't help. By 1905, local newspapers were still praising the feats of the local girls, but were also devoting space to the sport's critics.

"In a basket ball game, girls make the life of the official a dreary existence with constant kicking," said one unnamed but "well known" physical education instructor in the January 26 *Portland Evening Express*. "When it comes to recklessness, and a total disregard for personal injuries, girls, in the heat of conflict, take far greater chances than boys. In basket ball, girls will plunge and dive with great danger, and no injury short of a sprained ankle can induce a girl to withdraw from a game."

By 1908, many parents were forbidding their daughters to play the game. The Amateur Athletic Union, which governed sports activities outside the purview of high schools or colleges, declared that it

This early example of sporting goods featured an adjustable hoop.

32

A History of Basketball for Girls and Women

James Sullivan

would never permit girls to take part in basketball games in public places. The AAU's head, James E. Sullivan, believed that such public displays spawned undesirable traits and led to the exploitation of women.

The basketball committee blamed the men coaching girls and women for the problems with women's basketball. The men, they theorized, either ignored the women's rules or, while playing within them, encouraged rough and unladylike play. Men were more competitive than women and fostered this trait in their teams, the critics argued. Competitiveness, the committee decided, developed dangerous tendencies in women and a loss of grace, dignity, poise, and charm.

Agnes R. Wayman, a member of the committee, suggested that coaches, male and female, emphasize the feminine traits of their players on and off the court. She suggested making sure players kept their hair neatly combed, did not chew gum, use slang, or sit on the floor. Such things as pulling hair, kicking, slapping, and any displays of temper were to be considered unsportsmanlike conduct. The rules committee also made it a foul for coaches to shout encouragement or holler instructions to their players during the game, either for fear of upsetting or inciting the players.

Two of the biggest differences between men's and women's basketball games, besides the court divisions, were the limited dribble and the restrictions on guarding. Both of these rules were devised to make the game seem more feminine.

Berenson and her colleagues on the committee agreed that placing a limit on dribbling would foster sharing and equal opportunity for all the players on the court. They had seen how Naismith's unlimited dribbling rules had created star players who hogged the ball—definitely an unladylike characteristic. Still, the rules committee couldn't decide how many dribbles made sense. The committee completely eliminated dribbling in 1910 but restored one dribble to the game in 1913 because of complaints that the game was stagnant and unimaginative.

Defensive restrictions were also meant to provide equal opportunity among players of different heights and skill levels. That is, if a taller player could break the vertical plane in guarding an opponent, she would be able to block a shot or a pass more easily. Players took advantage of the guarding rule by perfecting the two-handed, overhead pass or shot, a maneuver that was almost impossible to guard against. For a time, the rules committee decided that the two-handed, overhead shot was only worth one point instead of two because it was impossible to block unless a defender broke the vertical plane.

Schools addressed concerns about girls getting too competitive by limiting the number of games played against teams from other schools. A basketball season often consisted of two to four games with other schools. The rest of the season was devoted to intramural games between classes of the same school. By 1912, some school yearbooks noted that women were only playing basketball against classmates rather than rival schools. Newspaper articles described the women's dress and manner on the court rather than the quality of their play.

Senda Berenson, who married a fellow Smith College faculty member and became Senda Abbott in 1911, believed she and the rules committee had saved women's basketball by making sure those who played and coached the game adhered to social conventions and acceptable behavior. Abbott retired from Smith College after she married in order to devote more time to her husband, her home, and to traveling. She did not give up her seat on the rules committee, though, until 1918 because of her devotion to the women's game. She and other committee members believed that without separate rules, the women's game might well have lost its support from the physical education community and the public. As Senda Berenson saw it, she had saved basketball for women.

The defender is abiding by the rule against breaking the vertical plane while guarding an opponent.

4

The Roller Coaster of the Roaring '20s

Basketball—and the girls who played it—epitomized the freer, anything-goes attitudes of the '20s, when the lively Charleston replaced the slower Tango as the decade's signature dance. Women finally had earned the right to vote in 1920. Their hard-won victory gave women confidence to express their beliefs and desires in other arenas. The '20s featured daredevil women such as Gertrude Ederle, the first woman to swim the English Channel in 1926, and Amelia Earhart, the solo pilot who grabbed headlines with her flights around the globe.

At many high schools, girls basketball was eclipsed in the mid-1920s only by football in the number of fans who cheered rabidly at games and followed the team faithfully. Girls who played basketball were often among the most popular in their classes. Yearbooks hailed them as conquering heroines playing for the sake of their school. Beside the

Opposite page: Basketball's popularity grew in the 1920s.

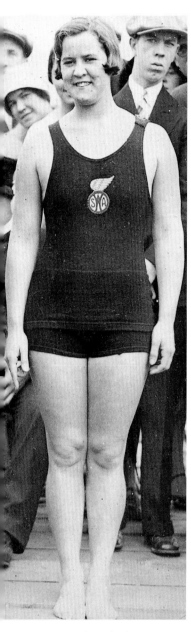

Gertrude Ederle

photo of Frances E. Johnson of Portland, Maine, the 1926 Deering High School yearbook editors wrote: "Here's to the fighting captain of the champion girls' basketball team. To a captain that has given her all for four full years to the honor and glory, not of herself, but of her school. Would that there were more who played the game as hardly and squarely as our Fran."

The Deering High girls, under the guidance of coach Ann McKechnie, captured the imagination of fellow students and townspeople as they reeled off long winning streaks and were proclaimed state champions for most of the decade. McKechnie, a biology teacher at the newly constructed high school, came of age in the years after the turn of the century. The daughter of Scottish immigrants, McKechnie devoted her life to serving girls and women as a teacher, a volunteer with the YWCA, and a summer camp counselor.

McKechnie had played shooting forward for Thornton Academy in Saco, which won the state championship in 1906. The team boarded a train to Lowell, Massachusetts, 100 miles to the south, for the New England championship. The teams played 15-minute halves, with six players on a side. As it was elsewhere, the ball was returned to the center jump after every basket. Thornton Academy didn't fare well against Lowell's taller girls because of that center jump rule, losing by the lopsided score of 55–2. McKechnie scored her team's only two points.

By the time McKechnie started coaching Deering in 1921, the girls were playing an ambitious schedule of games all over southern Maine. Newspaper columnists called McKechnie a brilliant coach who devised intricate plays, such as the block play that we call screening, and worked with her tall players to excel at what we call low-post play. McKechnie also ensured that her high school teams would keep winning by scouting elementary school teams and working with the most promising players early on.

"She took special care of the players when they got to high school," wrote Dorothy Hamlin in *The Maine Sunday Telegram* in November 1949 upon

McKechnie's death. "In talking with her players, we find they were all impressed with her ability to . . . bring out the best in them."

Iowa held its first state tournament for high school girls in 1920. Players recall using hand signals because they weren't supposed to talk to each other. The court was divided into thirds, and the ball was returned to the center jump after every score. People traveled long distances to see the girls play. Their games were more popular than boys games.

In nearby Minnesota, high school teams followed the train tracks to find opponents all over the wide, mostly rural state of the 1920s. The boys and girls teams usually traveled together, and whole towns sometimes turned out to greet them when the train pulled in to the station. Often, the teams played in dance halls with low ceilings because there was no gym in town. Local townspeople fed the visitors dinner and gave them beds for the night. If there was no train to take them home, they rode in horse-drawn wagons, sleighs, or bobsleds.

High school basketball flourished in Texas in the mostly rural communities that made up its wide expanse in the early years of the 1900s. Texas girls began playing high school tournaments in 1906 and began competing in regional championships in 1910. In Kentucky, where many high schools didn't offer girls basketball until 1910, the girls "took to it like a thoroughbred at the starting gate," according to one educator. Playing mostly by boys rules, more than 50 high school girls teams participated in district tournaments in 1922 that led to a state basketball championship.

Basketball was just as popular outside the confines of public or private high schools in the '20s. In Chicago, the Roamer Girls, a team of African-Americans from the South Side, were the darlings of the local black press. The Roamers played in the women's division of the African-American basketball league in Chicago, a league that featured church and local club teams. Sol Butler, a World War I hero who had also starred in international track and field competitions among allied troops, coached the

The Roller Coaster of the Roaring '20s

This 1909 game took place on the campus of Iowa State University.

A History of Basketball for Girls and Women

Texas high school girls, like the team above, enjoyed public support in the 1920s.

Roamers. Watching the Roamer Girls and other women's teams in local church halls or recreation centers became a social event for the black urban communities of the '20s. When *The Chicago Defender,* the local black newspaper, polled its readers in 1927 on the city's most popular black athlete, five of the 17 vote-getters were women, including Virginia Willis of the Roamer Girls.

In Los Angeles, the YMCA hosted a recreational league for girls beginning in 1922. The Pasadena Athletic and Country Club formed a women's basketball team in 1925. The members were also part of the club's successful track team, which produced two women who competed in the 1928 Olympics.

Industrial leagues, teams of players sponsored by the companies they worked for, sprouted up all over the country. Oil companies, insurance firms, banks, and other companies began recruiting women right out of high school or in college to come to work for them and to play on their traveling basketball team. Texas became a hotbed of women's industrial league basketball in the '20s.

Before 1920, 92 percent of the workforce in America had worked more than 48 hours a week, according to industrial surveys. But by 1920, almost half of Americans were working fewer than 48 hours. Employers hoped that by filling their employees' leisure time with fun and games, they would inspire loyalty to the company. Such loyalty would make for more productive workers, and it might also convince employees that they didn't need to join labor unions, which were targeting factories as well as office workers at this time.

Successful company teams were also good advertising. The Traveler's Insurance Company of Hartford, Connecticut, sponsored a women's team that made its name well known all over New England. The Travelers played alumnae squads from regional colleges and industrial teams such as the Connecticut-based American Thread team and the Chase National Bank team of New York.

Some women's teams knew no bounds when it came to finding good competition. The Edmonton,

Alberta, Commercial Grads played home games outdoors because they had no gym. Yet they traveled
125,000 miles across Canada, the United States, and
Europe looking for competition. In the 25 years they
played, from 1915 to 1940, the Grads won 522
games and lost only 20. They won 14 Canadian
championships and once won 147 consecutive
games. In 1924, they won the European championship and were declared world champions when
they won a tournament in France. *The New York
Times* praised Edmonton's girls as "brilliant defensive" players who played a "scientific" game that
"rarely went wrong."

Amazingly, all 38 of the women who played for
the Grads over the years attended the same commercial high school in Edmonton. Their coach, John
Percy Page, built a four-level farm system that developed players from the high school to the traveling
team. Mostly teachers and secretaries, the women
who played for the Grads were admonished to act
like ladies at all times. Any player who married had
to retire.

Texans had taken to industrial league women's
basketball in such large numbers that by 1920, close
to 1,000 women were applying to play in Amateur
Athletic Union sanctioned tournaments. The AAU
had been all male for many years and in the early
1900s had taken a stand against girls playing sports
in public. But by the early 1920s, the AAU leader-
ship decided it needed some control not just over
women's basketball, but over the burgeoning field
of women's athletics. The AAU began sponsoring
tournaments. The first AAU national basketball
championship took place in Pasadena in 1926, and
more than 5,000 fans attended. The Pasadena
(California) Athletic and Country Club won the
inaugural tournament.

But even as girls and women enjoyed this golden
era of basketball fever, criticism became louder and
more insistent. The increasingly vocal debate in
the '20s focused on how competitive girls games had
become and how dangerous the win-at-all-costs
spirit was to the proper development of girls, both

Lou Henry Hoover

physically and mentally. When they viewed women's basketball, critics of the game did not see hundreds of healthy girls having a wonderful time. Instead, they saw an intense, highly charged atmosphere inhabited by young women who had lost all dignity and refinement. Dressed sometimes in shiny satin shorts and sleeveless shirts, these girls, the critics argued, were in danger of being exploited commercially and sexually by the men who ran the show. Women who taught girls in physical education fueled the debate.

Elizabeth Quinlan, a professor at Boston Teachers' College in the mid-1920s, decried the sight of girls "egged on by the taunts of howling, cheering crowds in gymnasiums, losing their tempers and swearing at their opponents." She knew of girls who fainted after games and were still upset emotionally days after a game. Dr. Margaret Mead, the anthropologist, was an unlikely critic. Her studies showed that games and sports sometimes substituted for child-rearing and might, therefore, be detrimental to society. A less surprising critic was Pope Pius XI, the worldwide leader of the Catholic Church. Pope Pius conveyed his disapproval of girls playing sports in public competitions several times during his 17-year reign, which began in 1922.

The most influential critic, however, was Lou Henry Hoover, head of the Girl Scouts of America in 1923 and the wife of President Herbert Hoover. Lou Henry Hoover was an independent woman who traveled widely, spoke five languages, and had earned a degree in geology at Stanford University. Through her work with the Girl Scouts, she had become an advocate of sports as a building block of good character. Like the physical education professors, she believed that highly competitive sports excluded too many girls from the benefits of physical activity and team play.

Hoover helped found the Women's Division of the National Amateur Athletic Foundation (WDNAAF), which held its first conference in 1923. At the 1923 conference and subsequent meetings, the group attacked competitive athletics, especially basketball. In 1925, the WDNAAF passed a resolution, 72–2, outlawing extramural competition, opposing gate receipts at women's games, all travel for women's teams, and all publicity about women's sports. The group was elated when the National Association of Secondary School Principals supported its resolution.

The principals' association pressured state high school sports associations to disband tournaments. The campaign against interscholastic competition was most successful in the Eastern states and in the large city schools where enough girls were interested in basketball to form successful intramural programs. But in largely rural states, such as Iowa, Texas, Oklahoma, Tennessee, and Maine, efforts to ban competition met with mixed results. Maine, which did not have an official state tournament in the '20s, actually started one in 1931 under the auspices of local school officials in Livermore Falls, a tiny community outside the mill city of Lewiston.

Bertha Teague, whose coaching career spanned 43 years, started her girls basketball program at Ada Byng High School in Oklahoma in spite of all the controversy in 1927. Teague's teams won eight state titles and 1,157 games over the next four decades.

Black colleges in the South also continued to encourage interscholastic rivalries. South Carolina Agricultural and Mechanical College and Alabama State Teachers College hosted high school tournaments for girls in the 1920s and '30s. Tuskegee Institute hosted the national black high school tournament for both boys and girls in the mid to late 1930s. The Philadelphia Tribune Girls, a team of black urban women led by tennis champion Ora Washington, toured throughout the South in the early 1930s because there was more competition there than in the Northeast.

School officials in Iowa and Texas tried to comply with the interschool ban but met grassroots resistance from fans of the game. In Texas, three rival organizations offered girls tournaments after the state athletic association stopped hosting a girls basketball tournament.

A college team from the 1920s

Texas and other states offered girls the chance to play basketball despite the concerns of some educators.

In Iowa, the High School Athletic Association voted to substitute volleyball for basketball and to end the state tournament system in 1925. Rural school administrators and the publisher of Des Moines's daily newspaper, *The Register,* fought back and started their own organization called the Iowa Girls High School Athletic Union. In 1926, 159 Iowa schools fielded girls teams in the new association, which oversaw tournament play at the county, sectional, and state level. Sportswriters from the two Des Moines newspapers managed the state tournament and officiated games while also writing about the event.

Meanwhile, the women's division railed on. A note in the 1926 University of Kentucky yearbook tells readers that the women's basketball team was disbanded that year. No explanation follows. Kentucky actually held on to its women's basketball team longer than many colleges and universities. By the end of the 1920s, only 12 percent of colleges sponsored varsity basketball teams.

In 1926, at its convention at the Hotel Astoria in New York City, the women's division went after the businesses, chambers of commerce, and church groups who were using girls basketball teams to improve their images. In her progress report to the 1926 convention, Lillian Schoedler, the division's executive secretary, likened the competitive girls basketball tournaments to the bathing beauty pageants that also became popular in the 1920s.

"It is certainly to be regretted that such institutions are forming so black a chapter in the story of girls' athletics and that institutions that ought to stand so strongly for high ideals and constructive standards are permitting so much that is undesirable or even harmful to take place . . . for the sake of increasing their constituency and public prestige," she wrote.

The women's division successfully pressured city officials in Wichita, Kansas, a hotbed of industrial league basketball, to cancel the AAU National Women's Basketball Tournament in 1927 and 1928. The cancellation led some business owners to disband their teams.

But the male-dominated industrial leagues remained exceedingly popular. In 1929, Wichita revived the national AAU tournament and added a beauty contest to the event. The 1930 tournament in Wichita included 28 teams from a dozen different states, including Texas, Arkansas, North Carolina, Nebraska, Tennessee, Georgia, Alabama, Indiana, and Oklahoma. *The New York Times* reported on the event, which included a parade down the main street of Wichita before the games began.

Still, being a basketball star was losing its luster in many parts of the country. Rachel Bryant, who went on to be a leader in women's physical education in the 1950s, taught high school and coached basketball in Mentor, Ohio, in 1929. She also played for a semi-professional basketball team sponsored by a local taxi company that traveled all around the Great Lakes. Bryant's playing career ended, however, when her county superintendent of schools came to a game. When he expressed concerns about how revealing her uniform was, Bryant dutifully quit the team rather than risk her job.

As the Roaring '20s came to a close, many female athletes were beginning to struggle with all the swirling, contradictory notions of what it meant to be a woman and a basketball player. The fame of one particular female basketball star did much to fuel the concerns and even to taint the image of women in sports in general and basketball in particular.

"It is certainly to be regretted that such institutions are forming so black a chapter in the story of girls' athletics. . . ."

5

BABE AND TEXAS LEAGUE BASKETBALL

Sports had always been a part of life for Mildred Ella Didrikson. Born in 1911, the daughter of Norwegian immigrants, she grew up with four sisters and three brothers in Beaumont, Texas, a town near the Gulf coast and about 70 miles east of Houston. Her brothers called her Babe, for Babe Ruth, because she hit so many home runs in their sandlot games.

By the time she was in high school, Babe's favorite sport was basketball. She stood about 5 feet, 5 inches, which in those days was tall enough to be a shooting forward on a basketball team. She was tough and wiry and not afraid to use her elbows near the basket. Her high school team, the Miss Royal Purples, didn't lose a game from 1927 to 1930 when she played.

"We were a terrific team," recalled a teammate, Lois "Pee Wee" Blanchette, in 1975. Blanchette played what she called "hustling forward." She was responsible for getting the ball from the defensive end to the offensive end in the three-court game

Opposite page: Basketball was just one of the sports that Babe Didrikson Zaharias mastered.

they played. "I fed her [Babe] perfectly," said Blanchette. "The boys wouldn't admit it but they liked the girls teams to play the same nights as they did because we brought such big crowds."

Word of the Miss Royal Purples spread 250 miles northwest to Dallas. Employers Casualty Insurance Company had decided in 1924 that sponsoring championship industrial league sports teams was the best way to distinguish itself in the increasingly crowded home, auto, and personal insurance markets. Melvin Jackson McCombs, known as Colonel because of his stint in the army, was the athletic director and sometime coach of the company's women's athletic teams. McCombs was also a manager in the farm and cyclone insurance division, so his teams were called the Golden Cyclones.

By the late 1920s, the Golden Cyclones were one of the two best teams in the Dallas industrial league. Between 1,000 and 2,000 fans flooded into the Fair Park Automotive Building in Dallas to watch the Cyclones square off against such teams as Franklin Motor Car, Piggly Wiggly, and Sunoco Oil. Other fans tuned into the games on their radios.

In 1927 and 1928, the Sunoco Oilers were the superior team. They didn't lose a game all season and were declared the AAU national champions both years, though no national tournament was held. In 1929, the Cyclones finally beat the Oilers in a regular-season game. The Oilers took revenge at the AAU national championship, beating the Cyclones by a single point.

McCombs figured that if the Cyclones had just one more all-star in their lineup, they could win the tournament in 1930. So he traveled to Houston in February to scout the Royal Purples. McCombs saw Didrikson score 26 points as her Beaumont team defeated the much taller Houston Heights team. After the game, he talked to her father about hiring her to play for Employers Casualty.

The Didriksons gave their daughter permission to leave school for two months that year. Her father accompanied her on the train ride to Dallas where McCombs picked them up at the station in his big yellow Cadillac. McCombs gave her a clerical job and paid her $75 a month, or about $900 a year. Compared to coal miners and the average typist, who made $600 to $750 a year, the basketball players were making good money.

Babe's uniform was a shiny blue-and-white sleeveless shirt with belted plaid shorts as short as a swimsuit. She picked a shirt with the number 7 on it and a pair of skintight pants because she liked the look and feel of them. "There wasn't an ounce of fat on me," she recalled in her autobiography, *This Life I've Led.*

The Cyclones played a slightly different game than Babe had been playing in high school. During the '20s, the men who ran the AAU leagues decided to change from the three-court game that Berenson and Baer had invented to a two-court game. The two-court game was faster and quicker and more fun to watch, the AAU officials reasoned.

The Miss Royal Purples

A History of Basketball for Girls and Women

Didrikson quickly learned how to throw the javelin for gold medals.

In her first game that very night, and despite the fact that she hadn't even practiced with the Cyclones, Babe scored 14 points as the Cyclones won, 48–18. The Cyclones had two all-America forwards and two all-America guards. They defeated city league teams by scores of 82–5 and 62–9 that spring as they prepared for the AAU national tournament in Wichita. Babe was scoring 30 points a game some nights. She made 57 out of 65 shots to win the citywide foul-shooting contest.

Within three weeks, rival Kansas City Life Insurance Company offered Babe $80 a month plus bonuses of $25 to $100 a victory. But Babe was happy where she was. The Cyclones made it to the AAU championship and faced Sunoco Oil in front of 5,000 fans. Late in the game, Babe missed a foul shot that would have tied the score. The Cyclones lost by one point, but Babe was named to the all-America team.

Dallas newspapers covered 48 girls and women's basketball teams in 1930 but they showcased Didrikson. In one photo spread that Babe saved and sent to a friend back home in Beaumont, headshots of Babe's teammates form a circle around a larger photo of her "blown up way big." Other articles called her "Mighty Mildred."

"Man, I just loved that," she wrote in her autobiography, *This Life I've Led.*

Didrikson finished high school in Beaumont that May and returned to Dallas to work for Employers Casualty. She played softball and track and field while she awaited another basketball season. Babe had never even seen a javelin before. By the end of that summer, she set national records in the javelin and baseball throw and southern AAU records in the high jump, shot put, and the long jump.

When the 1931 basketball season rolled around, Didrikson led the Cyclones to the national championship. But by the following fall, her teammates were anything but grateful to their star player. McCombs was increasingly frustrated in his dealings with her, too. He had raised her salary to $90 a month, almost as much as the average teacher or

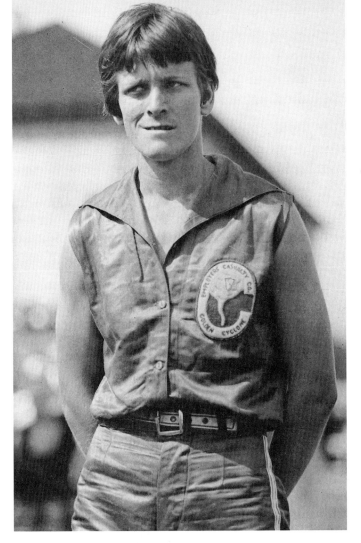

*Babe's athletic prowess
was indisputable but her
appearance and
personality were
controversial.*

steelworker was making in 1932. But Didrikson
thought she deserved more money. As a protest, she
refused to shoot the ball when she played.
McCombs ordered her benched. Her teammates
were disgusted, and some refused to room with her
on road trips because of her arrogance.

"She was masculine and she was an individual—
she was out for Babe, honey, just Babe," recalled
Mrs. Reagan Glen, who played with the Cyclones in
the early 1930s. "I admit I admired Babe because of
all the things she could do but some of the other
girls really resented her."

As her fame grew, the press responded to
Didrikson with a strange mixture of adulation and
ridicule. Local newspaper writers in Dallas and
Beaumont gushed about her accomplishments and

A History of Basketball for Girls and Women

Golf was the sport that finally provided Didrikson with an income.

her humble roots. But national sportswriters didn't know what to make of this working-class, tough-talking wonder woman who cut her hair short, wore no makeup, and considered girdles and stockings sissy attire. Magazines like *Colliers* and *Literary Digest,* which had run positive articles about women's basketball early on, began covering women's golf, tennis, and swimming instead. They wrote about the dresses the women wore and called the grown women who excelled at these more genteel sports "sweet little girls."

After her incredible performance in the 1932 Olympics in Los Angeles, where she took home two gold medals and a silver, some feature articles proclaimed Didrikson the greatest athlete in the world—ever. Others, though, focused on her masculine qualities and coarse manners.

"The image remains vivid of the geometric, bosomless, narrow-thin Texan with the hacked-off hair," wrote Betty Hicks, who grew up in the 1930s. "I had dreamed adolescent dreams of being a star athlete; now I saw what a woman athlete had to be."

Didrikson was forced to give up playing basketball for the Cyclones in 1933 because of charges that Chrysler had paid her to promote a car. But she continued to play basketball, joining a barnstorming team of men and women that crisscrossed the country playing games in small town gyms.

Dr. Belle Mead Holm, dean of the physical education department at Lamar University in Beaumont, grew up in the 1930s. She remembers signs tacked up in college gyms that read, "Don't be a muscle moll." That was the term sportswriter Paul Gallico had coined to describe Didrikson in a 1932 *Vanity Fair* article. Gallico had described Didrikson as an unhappy woman standing on the outside, looking on as her female peers chatted about hair, make-up, and boys.

This 1930s expectation—that athletes should maintain their femininity at all costs—was the catalyst for one of the most famous barnstorming basketball troupes in basketball history: the All-American Red Heads. In 1936, C.M. "Ole" Olson of Cassville,

Missouri, decided to form a team of women who would travel all over the country playing basketball. Olson's wife owned a chain of beauty salons in Missouri and Arkansas and knew how popular red hair was. She suggested calling the team the "Red Heads" and having them all dye their hair red and wear lipstick and makeup—at least for their publicity photos.

Olson recruited some of the best and the tallest amateur players—ones who liked the idea of performing the hidden ball trick, imitating the referee, shooting free throws from their knees, and playing piggyback while spinning the ball on the end of their fingers. Over the next three years, the Red Heads played as many as 200 games against men's teams all over the country, winning more than half of them. They drew hundreds of fans and were written about in *Ripley's Believe It or Not* and *Life* magazine.

If Babe Didrikson was ever invited to join the team, she didn't mention it in her autobiography or to anyone who wrote about her. By 1936, she had begun entering golf tournaments, a sport in which she could earn a living.

The Women's Division of the National Amateur Athletic Foundation, meanwhile, hammered away at competitive sports in the 1930s. Competitive girls basketball at the elementary, high school, and college level became almost invisible in many states across the country. Ohio banned tournaments for girls in 1930. The New York State High School Athletic Association ended high school tournaments in 1933. In 1937, Missouri voted to limit girls to one game a week and to eliminate tournament play.

By the beginning of the 1940s, the enthusiasm that had surrounded basketball for girls since the early 1900s had quieted down across most of the country. High school girls who still had teams to play for found themselves playing before empty bleachers and getting little notice by local newspapers.

Unless they were lucky enough to be living in Iowa.

Hazel Walker of the All-American Red Heads

24th annual

IOWA
Girls' High School Athletic Union
STATE BASKETBALL
CHAMPIONSHIP

DRAKE FIELDHOUSE
DES MOINES, IOWA

MARCH
1-2-3-4-5
1949

Official Program **25ᶜ**

6

BASKETBALL GROWS LIKE CORN IN IOWA

Cheers rang out as Helen Van Houten, Dorothy Crawford, and their Hansell High School teammates carried the 5-foot high state championship trophy into the gym Sunday afternoon. Many of the men, women, and children in the gymnasium had been among the 7,000 spectators at the Drake University Fieldhouse in Des Moines the previous night watching the Hansell High girls play the best game of their lives to defeat Waterville for the 1940 Iowa girls state basketball championship. The fans had formed a caravan of trucks, sedans, and station wagons that stretched a mile behind the school bus as it made its way back to town from Des Moines the next day.

Those who hadn't been able to leave their farms overnight or get tickets for the tournament listened to the results on the radio. Van Houten had scored 44 points in one of the crucial semifinal games of the tournament. In her four-year career, Van Houten scored more than 2,500 points. "The guard would get it over half court to me and I'd get it into the pivot to Helen," recalled Crawford, who still lived in

Opposite page: The program from the 1949 Iowa girls basketball tournament

"Gentlemen, if
you attempt
to do away
with girls'
basketball in
Iowa, you'll be
standing in
the center of
the track when
the train runs
over you."

Hansell in 1999. "She was tall and she could pivot both ways."

"It was one of those experiences you never forget," Van Houten said 12 years later in 1952. ". . . wanting something very badly and putting every effort into it. It's good to work hard for a good goal."

While victory was the crowning jewel, the trip to Des Moines itself had been the thrill of a lifetime for the Hansell girls. They had stayed in the Franklin Hotel downtown, eaten breakfast with the governor, toured the state house, bought their prom dresses with money they had saved up all year, and been interviewed and photographed for a four-page story and photo spread in *Life* magazine. Not bad for a group of farm girls who grew up shooting hoops off the side of their barns during breaks from detasseling ears of corn.

By 1940, winning the state championship was the dream of every girl who played basketball in Iowa. They didn't know that high school girls in most states could not dream such dreams. Even in places where high school basketball had once thrived, like Massachusetts, California, and New York, girls were playing a shadow season. Their season ended with the final regular-season game. The only recognition girls received for playing was a varsity letter for their sweaters. Some of the lucky ones got to show off their foul-shooting skills at a contest before the boys tournament.

Iowa girls could easily have suffered the same fate had it not been for four maverick school superintendents who formed the Iowa Girls High School Athletic Union (IGHSAU) in 1925. One founder, John W. Agans, stood up at the Iowa High School Athletic Association meeting in 1925 where 250 members voted to ban girls tournaments and said: "Gentlemen, if you attempt to do away with girls' basketball in Iowa, you'll be standing in the center of the track when the train runs over you."

If Agans was the Patrick Henry of Iowa girls basketball, M. M. McIntire was George Washington. McIntire moved to Iowa from Pennsylvania to become the school superintendent in Audubon, a small town in the southwestern corner of the state. He began coaching the girls team in 1921 and proceeded to lead Audubon to the state championship three years in a row, from 1921 to 1924.

McIntire thought his 1923 team was so good that he challenged the Texas champions, Guthrie High School, to a best-of-three-games series. Guthrie won the first two games easily and went on to claim the national championship by traveling to New York and New Jersey and beating good teams there.

McIntire and the other superintendents knew that girls basketball—and the goal of making it to the postseason tournament—was an important part of school and community life in rural Iowa. McIntire saw how tournament time opened up a whole new world to Iowa farm girls and their families. Overnight train trips afforded opportunities to make lifelong friends and meet new people while staying at opposing players' homes. He felt it would be unfair—not just to the girls but to the school and the whole community—to deprive them of the opportunities competitive basketball provided.

With publicity from the Des Moines newspapers and donations from local merchants, McIntire mobilized 159 school districts. Together, they kept the district, regional, and state tournaments going through the late '20s and the lean years of the Great Depression—when girls practiced in their stocking feet to save their sneakers for the real games. Even in the mid-1930s, when city schools in Des Moines, Dubuque, Ottumwa, and other larger communities caved into the pressure from the NAAF and banned girls basketball, the small-school union grew. By 1940, when Hansell—a town of 180 people—sent its girls to Des Moines for the tournament, 70 percent of the teams there came from schools of fewer than 100 students.

If parents and townspeople heard the criticism about girls playing basketball, they dismissed it as nonsense. They knew that their girls, many descended from German, Czech, Danish, and Swedish immigrants, could handle the strain

Girls basketball action from Iowa in the 1930s

A History of Basketball for Girls and Women

Iowa basketball players experimented with a white ball.

involved in running half the length of a basketball court. They had heard stories on many a winter night of how their mothers and grandmothers had played on chalk-lined or newly shoveled courts in the middle of main street or on grassy plots where the grass had been burned off. They heard tales of heroic early-tournament feats, like the time Correctionville played five games in two days in 1920 to win the first state championship at Drake University. They knew the names of legendary female players, such as Geneva and Jo Langerman, twin sisters who led their high school team to the state championship in 1931 and 1932. The Langermans then proceeded to lead their AAU team to the national championship in 1934 before joining the famous All-American Red Heads.

By 1940, a town's girls basketball games gave people a chance to get together for a night out. Planning the annual trip to Des Moines was for many people like planning a trip to Disney World. "They came down through blizzards to see us," recalled Dorothy Crawford.

Through the years of World War II, girls basketball continued to capture the imagination of small-town Iowa. The seamless ball, introduced in the late '30s, greatly improved play by the 1940s, as did the rule adopted in 1934 that divided the court into two equal parts instead of three. The seamless ball, which had an air pouch inside of it that could be inflated with an air pump, did not wear out or take unpredictable bounces the way the old balls had. With no third-of-an-inch high seams to contend with, the girls could grip the ball evenly. They developed new moves, such as the lay-up, the bounce pass, and the jump shot. Iowa schools also used an unusual white leather ball in the late 1930s and early '40s.

The rule change that divided the court into halves went into effect nationally at all levels of play in 1938, but Iowa had pioneered the change at the high school level in 1934 after the annual state coaches clinic. There, R. C. Bechtel, the coach of an AAU team based in Iowa, explained how the two-court rule eliminated the need for a center jump after every score. Instead, the opposing team got the ball at center court, thus speeding up the game and, in some cases, making it less lopsided if one team lacked a tall player at the center position.

Bechtel showed how both offensive and defensive strategy became more intricate with three guards playing against three forwards on either end of the court instead of two-on-two in three different areas of the court. Two weeks after the clinic, the school superintendents of the IGHSAU got together and voted to shift to the two-court game.

O. E. Lester coached four different teams in his 30-year career. While his teams never won the state championship, they almost always made it to the tournament in Des Moines where the best 16 teams in the state assembled for a showdown every March. Lester's teams were always well dressed, thanks to his wife Ruth. She designed 11 sets of uniforms for her husband's teams in the late 1940s and early '50s. By then, Iowa girls were wearing the same satin-cloth, sleeveless shirts and short shorts that Babe Didrikson's Golden Cyclones had popularized in the 1930s. Ruth Lester's radical contribution was a bare midriff shirt that tied in the front like a halter top, accompanied by a short, pleated skirt much like cheerleaders wore. Lester's outfits,

O. E. Lester's high school team of Oakland, Iowa, in 1949 wore splashy midriff tops.

The Girl Who Rarely Missed

A Maine schoolgirl took girls high school basketball out of the shadows—briefly—in the late 1940s, capturing the imagination of players, fans, and reporters beyond her tiny hometown of New Gloucester. Stella Waterman and her teammates won 73 games in a row in their four years of high school basketball.

Stella grew up on a dairy farm. At an early age, she fell in love with the game of basketball after her father tacked up a bushel basket inside the cow barn so that she, her sister, and her five brothers could play.

There were only 20 girls in the whole school when Waterman became a high school freshman. Fifteen of them were on the basketball team. From the beginning, Stella was their leader. She started grabbing newspaper headlines her sophomore year when she won the state's inaugural foul-shooting contest for girls in March of 1948.

During her junior year, word spread around southern Maine that this team was worth watching and that Stella, who was averaging close to 30 points a game, was especially worth watching. The problem with watching New Gloucester play was its gym—a tiny room on the second floor of the town hall. The wooden court was so small that the circles around center court and the foul line intersected at either end.

The restricted space became the ultimate home-court advantage for New Gloucester. Two well-placed passes were all that was needed  for an end-to-end fast break. Three hundred screaming fans in a space that should have held fewer than one hundred un-nerved a lot of opponents.

"The ball moved a lot faster between players," recalled Stella in 1998. "The strategy was to decoy your guard by playing deep and then coming back to get the ball."

By the middle of her senior year, Stella and the New Gloucester team were beating teams in their small-school league by scores of 102–42. In her senior year, Stella twice scored more than 60 points and averaged almost 40 points a game.

The Maine Secondary School Principals Association had banned girls tournaments, but coach Ray Stickney's phone kept ringing as coaches from other towns around the state inquired about playing exhibition games against New Gloucester.

Stickney said he wanted the games played in public so his team's fans could enjoy what he figured would be a well-played game, whether his team won or lost. A team from Richmond, a school just outside the state capital in Augusta, accepted the challenge and lost twice to New Gloucester by respectable margins of about 15 points in games played at a neutral site.

South Portland's coach, Eleanor Chambers, had been lobbying for years for a postseason tournament for girls. She told Stickney she'd be glad to have her squad play New Gloucester in front of a crowd at her gym, which had bleachers along one side of the court and a balcony that surrounded the court.

Newspapers from Bangor to Boston wrote about the upcoming David-Goliath battle between New Gloucester, a school of only 20 girls, against South Portland, whose female enrollment was 550. By the night of the game, tickets were long gone and people were turned away.

The lucky 1,100 in attendance saw New Gloucester get off to a slow start on the bigger court, about 22 feet longer than their own floor. After a couple of misses, Stella found her range with an assortment of hook shots and fadeaway jumpers. She wound up with 31 points as New Gloucester turned back South Portland's late rally and won the game, 48–40.

"Displaying court polish and maneuvers worthy of many a male basketeer, famed Stella Waterman proved almost unstoppable," wrote Vern Putney in *The Portland Press Herald* the next day.

Stella and her teammates celebrated their 73rd consecutive victory with ice cream sundaes at a Howard Johnson's restaurant on the way back to New Gloucester.

Stella ended her career with 2,161 total points. She averaged 26.6 points over her four years, and boosted her average to 38.7 points a game in her final year. In 20 of New Gloucester's 26 games that year, she outscored the opposing team by herself.

As Stella's high school career ended, Ole Olson asked her to join the All-American Red Heads. But Stella's parents weren't in favor of her joining the team, and she was apprehensive about being away from home for months at a time.

Stella became a successful college basketball and field hockey coach. But she will always be remembered best in New Gloucester as the girl who rarely missed on the team that never lost.

introduced in 1946, drew some criticism from people who thought they exploited the girls and took the focus off the game. The styles soon caught on all over the state, though, adding glamour and color to the game.

By 1946, most Iowa newspapers were covering regular-season games all over the state in the weeks leading up to the state tournament. Sixteen Iowa papers carried a syndicated column by Rod H. Chisholm about Iowa girls basketball called "The Queens of the Court." Nine radio stations set up broadcast booths at the state tournament in 1946. In 1947, the famous sportswriter and sports broadcaster Red Barber interviewed Gene Shumate, a Des Moines radio commentator, about Iowa girls basketball on Barber's nationally syndicated radio show.

"The states which do not permit girls high school basketball do so on the grounds that the competition would spoil a girl's femininity," Shumate told Barber. "We can't agree with that in Iowa. We've taken to our hearts these lassies who play all out, race madly hither and yon, but still remember to pause in the midst of a scoring rally to adjust a hair ribbon. We think it's the greatest show on earth."

After Iowa girls graduated from high school, many kept on playing basketball. Most liberal arts colleges across the country were still offering only intramural basketball, but Iowa Wesleyan College decided in 1943 to field a competitive women's team in response to public demand. The school's football and men's basketball coach, Olan Ruble, was recruited to coach the women. Within two years, Ruble had the Wesleyan Tigerettes competing in regional AAU tournaments.

By the mid-1940s, the AAU had expanded into a network of leagues and teams all over the South and Midwest. Former Iowa high school stars made powerhouses out of such AAU teams as the American Institute of Commerce "Stenos" in Davenport, Iowa, and Dr. Swett's Root Beer based in Des Moines.

The AIC Stenos earned their nickname because most of the women were preparing for careers as secretaries or stenographers. They proved to be as handy with a basketball as they were with a pen, winning the AAU national championship in 1942 and 1943. Six different Stenos made the AAU all-America team in those two years, including Frances Stansberry, a 5-foot-9 shooter from the tiny town of Farson. She could shoot with either hand and is considered Iowa's first jump shooter. When she played forward, fans called her "Stansberry the Unstoppable." When she switched to guard, they called her "Stansberry the Stopper."

Like the Edmonton Commercial Grads in Canada, the AIC Stenos were among the handful of women's teams that pioneered international play. During World War II, the Stenos raised $40,000 by playing exhibition games in Toronto, Canada. The money helped British children who had been left homeless by the war. In 1943, the Stenos traveled to Mexico for a 21-day basketball tour where they raised money to buy sewing machines for needy Mexican women. In 1949, the Stenos logged 7,000 miles during a goodwill tour of South and Central America to teach girls the game of basketball.

Even if basketball wasn't a ticket out of the country for Iowa high school graduates, it often was a ticket to the big city and the first step into careers in nursing, publishing, or insurance. Such diverse businesses as the Maytag Company in Newton and *Look* magazine, Northwestern Bell, Armstrong Tire, and Meredith Publishing in Des Moines vied for the best talent. "If you want to go right on playing basketball, if you like to bowl, play softball or tennis, you'll find all those things in the recreational program at Maytag," one of its magazine ads read.

Even girls who quit playing to raise families, like Dorothy Crawford, say they treasure the memories of their basketball-playing days. "I still remember how, before the games, we went over to the restaurant across the street and they gave us [free] orange juice with honey in it," said Crawford in 1998 as she reminisced about her girlhood days on that championship team in 1940. "We were a rough and tumble team. We just lived to play basketball."

"We just lived to play basketball."

7

THE AAU ERA

Eckie Jordan grew up in Pelzer, South Carolina, and started playing basketball in the fifth grade. She led her high school team to the state championship in 1942. After high school, Jordan played with one of the local teams in the textile mill league. She became engaged to a local man, but the relationship didn't work out. So Jordan decided in 1948 to head northeast to Winston-Salem, North Carolina, where the owner of Hanes Hosiery was recruiting players for a women's basketball team.

"My daddy loved basketball but he wasn't sure I should move so far away," recalled Jordan 51 years later. "I cried for weeks, I was so homesick. Five hundred miles might as well have been a million in those days."

Hanes had built a gymnasium for its men's and women's basketball teams so the players could practice after their 8 A.M. to 4 P.M. shifts in the hosiery mill. Still, teammates often played outside during their lunch break on one of the dirt courts near the mill. The women's team scrimmaged regularly against local high school boys teams and sometimes practiced until 9 at night to prepare for the upcoming season. League play began in November. Fellow textile workers and townspeople paid 25 cents and packed the gymnasium to see the team play. Even after the war ended, the industrial plants continued

Opposite page: Note the formal attire of the spectators at this 1948 game.

A History of Basketball for Girls and Women

Although the action was vigorous, the uniforms still focused on modesty.

to sponsor women's basketball teams because they had become so much a part of life in the mill towns and cities. "Very few days go by that we don't see someone who tells us how much they enjoyed watching us play," says Jordan, who still lived in Winston-Salem in 1999.

Jordan was a quick, 5-foot-2 ball-handler who played roving guard. Her ball-handling skills and off-balance shots made her the perfect complement to 6-foot-2 teammate Eunies Futch, who joined the team in 1947. Futch grew up in Jacksonville, Florida, where the high school didn't have a girls basketball team. Hanes Hosiery recruited her in 1947 while she was still in the 11th grade. Futch left school and Jacksonville to "go big time," as she recalled 52 years later.

Many Midwestern and Southern girls found opportunities to play basketball after high school, thanks to the Amateur Athletic Union and industrial league teams. Some estimate that close to 10,000 companies sponsored sports programs for their workers in the 1940s. Hanes and other elite AAU teams such as Cooks Goldblum, a brewery in Nashville; Dr Pepper, a soft drink company in Arkansas; and the Atlanta Blues, an independent team from Georgia, scheduled most of their games against each other during the regular season. That meant spending most every weekend on the road, traveling by bus, train, station wagon, and sometimes plane to play. The season culminated in the AAU national tournament, which by 1951 was a weeklong festival that showcased the best female players in the country and attracted thousands of fans.

The AAU tournament continued to highlight society's ambivalence toward its female athletes. While the games were highly competitive and featured as much roughness as the six-player rules allowed, players were admonished to dress well and look their best at all times. A beauty contest was also part of the tournament festivities. "We were always more interested in the free-throw contest," recalled Eckie Jordan. "As far as the beauty contest, that didn't impress us . . . but if they wanted it, OK."

By 1951, coach Virgil Yow had turned the seamstresses and office workers of Hanes Hosiery into AAU national champions. Hanes won 102 games in a row on its way to three straight national championships in 1951, 1952, and 1953.

"They gave us three free pairs of silk hose after our trips and in those days hose were expensive," says Futch, who lived in Winston-Salem in 1999. "I would guess we had even more fun than girls have playing today. We just loved to play."

The team that finally ended Hanes Hosiery's win streak in February 1954 was Wayland Baptist College, a small coed school tucked away in the Texas panhandle town of Plainview. Wayland Baptist had had a women's basketball team since the 1920s, but until 1948 its schedule was limited to playing high school teams. Then, in an effort to increase the school's enrollment by attracting more women, the school president urged coach Sam Allen to offer scholarships and to schedule games with AAU teams in Dallas and San Angelo. The school's athletic director, Harley Redin, who also coached the men's team, began tutoring the women in his spare time.

The basketball program got a big boost in 1951 when a generous alumnus of the college, Claude Hutcherson, decided to sponsor the team. Hutcherson, a wealthy Texas rancher who owned the local airport, loaned the school four Beechcraft Bonanzas so that the women's team could fly to an exhibition game in Mexico. Hutcherson and Redin each piloted a plane. After the trip, Hutcherson decided that the next season the team should travel to all its games in the four-passenger Beechcrafts. To acknowledge his generosity, the college changed the team's nickname from the Wayland Harvest Queens to the Hutcherson Flying Queens. At the national AAU tournament in March, the Flying Queens made it to the finals for the first time but lost to Hanes Hosiery.

Wayland Baptist had little trouble recruiting talented players. The idea of traveling by plane instead of bus and the prospect of trips to Mexico City,

"I would guess we had even more fun than girls have playing today. We just loved to play."

Nashville, Little Rock, Atlanta, and other cities that hosted AAU teams and tournaments attracted some of the best players in Texas, Oklahoma, and Missouri. Among them were hook-shot artist Ruth Cannon of tiny Cotton Center, Texas, who would become the Queens' all-time scoring leader during her four years at Wayland, and the Wilson twins, Faye and Raye, two defensive standouts from Duncanville, Texas.

By the time Harley Redin, the school's athletic director, took over as coach in 1955, Cannon and the Wilson sisters had led the Queens to two national titles and a 52-game winning streak. The school president declared a campus holiday and the town of Plainview celebrated with a parade when the team returned from the AAU tournament in 1955.

In 1955, Hanes Hosiery disbanded its women's basketball team when the company president retired and coach Yow left to coach a men's college basketball team. Eunies Futch and Eckie Jordan ended their careers in style, though. They were named to the first national team that would represent the United States in the international Pan Am Games held in Mexico City in the summer of 1955. (The AAU had been sending all-star teams to tournaments outside the country since 1953.) The U. S. team was coached by Caddo Matthews, the coach of Wayland Baptist College before Redin, and won the gold medal with an 8-0 record. It was the closest thing to an Olympic gold medal that American women could claim.

"It still gives me the chills," said Jordan in 1999. "There were 100,000 people in the stands for the opening ceremonies. It was a wonderful feeling to know you were representing your country."

With Hanes Hosiery out of the picture, the Hutcherson Flying Queens extended their win streak to 76 games and won their third national championship in 1956. Despite their dominance, the Flying Queens' winning streak and national title earned little more than a two-line paragraph in the sports section of many local papers across the country. The championship drew the attention of *Sports*

Illustrated magazine a few weeks later. Its story in April 1956 began by pointing out that girls at most colleges "seem more inclined to dream of hitting it rich in Hollywood than of sinking the old casaba from outside the foul line."

The story credited booster Claude Hutcherson's generosity for the team's success. It concluded with an example: "Claude Hutcherson is still the team's No. 1 fan," the article stated. "Before this year's tournament at St. Joseph, Missouri, he hired a nationally recognized hair stylist to give the team that look of chic so necessary to feminine morale."

The Flying Queens' goals for 1957 were to win a fourth national title and surpass the 101-game winning streak record that Hanes Hosiery had set in 1954. While Hanes Hosiery and Nashville Business College had built successful teams around individual star players, Harley Redin developed a strategy that involved all the players and revolutionized the six-player game.

AAU games were played with two guards, two forwards, and two rovers who could roam the whole court, playing both offense and defense. Redin taught his guards to get the rebound out to one of the rovers, who quickly passed to the other rover cutting over half court to start a three-on-two and sometimes a four-on-two fast break that left the opponent's defenders wondering what hit them. "We believed in running," said Redin in 1998. "That was our trademark."

The Flying Queens broke the AAU record for consecutive wins and won their fourth national championship by defeating Iowa Wesleyan College, 36–33. Harley Redin was invited to coach the U. S. team in the World Championship tournament that summer in Rio de Janeiro. When the tournament was postponed to October, Redin and the six Flying Queens named to the team backed out, fearing it would interfere with schoolwork and their upcoming AAU season. The U. S. team rallied from a three-point deficit at halftime to defeat the Soviet Union, 51–48, for the world championship.

A History of Basketball for Girls and Women

Nera White

"They are the strongest and roughest I've ever played against," Lucille Davidson, one of the players from Kansas City, wrote of the Soviets in her diary. Davidson, at 33, was the oldest member of the team. "When the final whistle blew, we all went crazy . . . This was our Olympics."

The Flying Queens made it to the national AAU tournament again in 1958, with a winning streak of 129 games. But in the semifinals, the Flying Queens finally lost to Nashville Business College, 46–42, to end their streak at 131 games, still the longest winning streak in AAU or women's collegiate basketball.

The Flying Queens continued to be formidable opponents and placed several players on U. S. teams that traveled abroad for the world championships and the Pan Am Games. But as the 1960s dawned, Nashville Business College—led by Nera White and Joan Crawford—became the team to beat.

White grew up in Lafayette, Tennessee, on a farm in the middle of tobacco country. Nashville Business College recruited White out of high school in 1955. Nashville's coach, John Head, was impressed with her 6-foot-1 frame, her dribbling and shooting skills, and her quickness. She could control the boards, dunk the ball, and run the floor faster than anyone else. "She was incredibly quick and fast," said Sue Gunter, a former teammate of White's who coached the 1980 Olympic team. "You saw guys do things she did, but not women."

White actually attended Peabody College for Teachers but the team paid her room and board. After graduation, Nashville's sponsor, H. O. Balls, hired White to work in his printing shop. Her pay was only $1 an hour, but she continued to earn her wage while playing games and practicing.

During their playing days together, White got most of the headlines, but teammates respected Crawford's work ethic as much as her basketball skills. Almost 6 feet, she led the team in rebounds every year and was the team MVP in 1963 and 1964. "Joan was that blue-collar worker who pounded it in, day in and day out," recalled Gunter.

Crawford was born in Fort Smith, Arkansas, with a birth defect that made it impossible for her to make the "s" sound. "I let my ball-playing talk for me," she said in 1997, the year she was inducted into the Naismith Memorial Basketball Hall of Fame. Crawford led her high school to three state championships, and Nashville Business College recruited her to be the other rover beside Nera White.

With White and Crawford leading the offense, Nashville won 10 national titles. White was named an all-American for 15 straight years, Crawford for 13. They not only led Nashville to all those titles, but they also led the U. S. team to the gold medal at the World Championship tournament in Brazil in 1957, where White was selected the best basketball player in the world.

Wayland Baptist's Hutcherson Flying Queens set records in the 1950s that stood for 50 years.

Hazel Walker and the Arkansas Travelers

Some say that Hazel Walker, who grew up in Oak Hill, Arkansas, was the best female basketball player ever. She played for AAU teams for 14 years in the 1930s and early 1940s, the barnstorming Red Heads in the mid-1940s, and started her own team in 1949. Yet few people have heard of Hazel or her Arkansas Travelers.

Hazel began playing basketball in the late 1920s at the age of 14. As a senior in high school, she led her Ashdown High School team to Arkansas's first state championship for girls. Ashdown lost the championship game by a point, but Hazel was named to the all-star team. A tall, striking young woman of Cherokee descent, Hazel also was voted most beautiful girl in the tournament.

Hazel received a full scholarship to play for Tulsa Business College after high school. She led Tulsa to a national championship and proceeded to play on three more championship teams during her 14 years of AAU competition. She won six national free throw contests and was named to 11 all-America teams. In 1946, Ole Olson lured Hazel away from the amateur ranks onto the All-American Red Heads, the professional team he'd started in 1936. Hazel didn't want to dye her hair red, so she wore a red wig instead. Hazel

found that she liked making money playing basketball. She didn't mind all the traveling the Red Heads did as they challenged a different men's team in a different town or city every night. But Hazel didn't like the fact that the Red Heads sometimes tried to get their opponents and the referees to take it easy on them.

"The thing that bothered me was they wanted a set up," she said before her death in 1990. "They didn't want the men to call fouls too closely on us."

In 1949, Hazel decided to start her own team, Hazel Walker's Arkansas Travelers, who would play a more serious brand of basketball while still entertaining the fans. Hazel held tryouts and chose the seven players who she felt exhibited the best combination of good character, neatness, attractiveness, and ability.

While society had accepted women as construction workers, shipbuilders, pilots, and athletes during the war years, the 1950s saw a change in attitude toward women workers and athletes. As in the 1930s, the ability to adhere to ideals of womanly attractiveness and nurturing qualities again became more prized than the can-do spirit of the war years. Hazel felt her team would be more accepted if her players accentuated their feminine qualities while still playing hard.

Frances "Gus" Garroutte, one of the original Travelers, recalled how Hazel warned players to dress nicely and to act like ladies when they were in public to counter the idea that they were "trash."

"[The fans] expected a bunch of rough-looking women and they were always surprised," said Garroutte. "We helped people understand that you can look like a lady, act like a lady, and still play ball."

With money she'd saved from her three-year stint with the Red Heads, Hazel bought a station wagon with a luggage rack on top and started scheduling games.

Wherever they went, the Arkansas Travelers challenged the best male athletes in town to games and played by men's rules. They played six nights a week and often drove to the next stop after they'd split the gate receipts with the

home team.

To ward off robbery attempts, the Travelers carried a gun with them, "and we weren't afraid to use it," said Garroutte.

The Travelers showed a generation of little girls in the 1950s and early 1960s that women could lead independent lives and be as good at basketball as any man. In 16 seasons of play, the Travelers won 85 percent of their games. Hazel was said to have won every halftime free throw shooting contest during those 16 years.

"To see her play, to see that women could be that good, it changed me forever," said Elva Bishop, a documentary filmmaker for North Carolina Public Television. She saw Walker play in her hometown of Aberdeen, North Carolina, and went on to make a documentary film about the pioneers of the women's game.

Walker retired at the age of 50 in 1965. The Arkansas Travelers retired with her.

A History of
Basketball for Girls
and Women

*The 1958 U. S. national
team*

White wasn't just a scoring machine. Though she could hit a jump shot or hook shot from 30 feet away, she took pride in her rebounding and assists. In 1962, as Nashville Business College sought to win back the AAU national title from Wayland Baptist, White found herself being double- and triple-teamed as she drove to the basket against the Flying Queens' collapsing defense. She scored only eight points that night but grabbed 14 rebounds and handed out 11 assists, many of them to Crawford. Nashville won the national championship in 1962 and began a dynasty of eight straight titles from 1962 to 1969. The team reeled off 96 wins in a row.

"She cared more about and took more pride in helping a teammate get open, to get the open shot, than she cared about scoring herself," said former teammate Doris Rogers of White. "She was the most talented player I'd ever seen."

White's and Crawford's careers ended in 1969 when the AAU decided to switch to the five-player game. H. O. Balls opposed the change and chose to disband the team. White, 33, and Crawford, 32, could still have run the court with anyone but they chose to retire. Crawford moved to Chicago where she landed a job at the Northwestern University Library. White adopted the child of an unmarried former teammate and returned to Tennessee to farm.

In the years since, highways and gymnasiums in Tennessee were named after White. She became the first of two women inducted into the Naismith Memorial Basketball Hall of Fame in Springfield, Massachusetts, in 1992 and one of the first 25 women inducted into the Women's Basketball Hall of Fame, which opened in 1999.

Crawford got into the Hall of Fame in Springfield five years later and also was among the first 25 women in the Women's Basketball Hall of Fame. But because they played in the shadows of the 1950s and 1960s, when newspapers gave two-paragraph mentions to women's basketball, few people know about White and Crawford, women who began to play the game—almost—the way Naismith intended.

8

A TIME OF CHANGE

In politics, music, and everyday life, the 1960s were a time of tremendous upheaval. Attitudes toward women in society and the workplace were changing. President John F. Kennedy's commission on the Status of Women, chaired by former first lady Eleanor Roosevelt, was one catalyst for social change. In 1962, Roosevelt's commission called for legislation to ensure women equal opportunity and equal pay.

A 1963 book by Betty Friedan, *The Feminine Mystique,* approached the problem of women's aspirations from a different angle. Friedan was a Smith College graduate who gave up a career as a psychologist to raise three children. She interviewed dozens of women who had given up their own ambitions and talents for marriage and motherhood. Friedan, who later left her husband because he physically abused her, described the women she interviewed as frustrated and unfulfilled.

Friedan's book was a lightbulb for many American women. Like Friedan, they had given up work or were working in jobs that paid half of what men earned and did not fully use their skills or their intelligence. Friedan's ideas also touched a nerve

Opposite page: Lusia Harris was one of the first stars of women's college basketball.

among social activists who likened women's struggles to that of blacks in society.

By 1964, two laws—the Equal Pay Act and Title VII of the Civil Rights Act—had been passed, expanding the rights of women. By 1968, the National Organization for Women (NOW) was lobbying for an Equal Rights Amendment. That summer, 200 women took to the streets of Atlantic City outside the convention hall where the Miss America Pageant was being staged. In a symbolic act, they tossed bras, girdles, hair curlers, and false eyelashes into a trash can and set them on fire. Their actions captured front-page headlines across the country and symbolically ignited the women's liberation movement.

Women's basketball also changed dramatically. In the early 1960s, the American Medical Association, which had cautioned against strenuous competition for girls, began endorsing vigorous activity. President Kennedy emphasized physical fitness for

Protestors picket in front of the site of the 1968 Miss America pageant.

all school children. The Cold War—in which the United States and the Soviet Union vied for supremacy in space exploration, scientific achievement, and in Olympic-level athletic competition—also changed attitudes toward the highly skilled female athlete.

Katherine Ley, a leader with the Division of Girls and Women in Sports of the American Association for Health, Physical Education and Recreation, urged the DGWS Executive Council to "train the best we had to perform to the best of their ability. At the same time, promote all sports for all girls and women so that eventually we will have more prospects [for the Olympics] from which to choose."

Thus, in the mid-1960s, varsity sports programs for girls and women emerged at many high schools and colleges. By the end of the 1960s, 80 percent of all colleges had extramural competition in many sports, including basketball. Fifty percent of high schools across the country had interscholastic teams.

These programs did not get the same level of funding from athletic departments as the boys or men's programs, though. The players often held bake sales, car washes, and raffles to buy uniforms or warm-up jackets. Coaches received only a token stipend and often used their own money for transportation, food, entry fees, and sometimes even to pay the officials. Most schools did not allot gym time evenly. Sometimes, if a girls game went on too long, it was suspended so that the boys' practice could start on time.

Betty Friedan

High school girls were still playing the two-court game without any rovers in 1960, although college and AAU games and tournaments used rovers. The DGWS rules committee finally instituted experimental rules employing two rovers in 1961 despite protests from physical educators who feared, as their foremothers had, that men would take over the sport.

Slowly, physical education leaders made the changes that brought the women's game more in line with the men's game. In 1966, the unlimited dribble became official. In 1969, the five-player

A History of Basketball for Girls and Women

Billie Jean Moore, Cal State-Fullerton coach

game was instituted on an experimental basis, along with the 30-second shot clock. The DGWS expected lots of criticism during the two-year trial period, but surprisingly few people protested. More than 90 percent of physical educators who answered questionnaires said they favored the five-player game.

By 1966, so many colleges had initiated competitive sports programs that physical education instructors decided to create a Commission on Intercollegiate Athletics to oversee national tournaments for women in basketball and other sports. This commission led to the Association for Intercollegiate Athletics for Women (AIAW), which began in the fall of 1967. The National Collegiate Athletic Association (NCAA), which oversaw men's collegiate sports, had no interest in women's programs. That was fine with women physical educators. They thought the NCAA was an overly commercial operation too beholden to alumni, sponsors, and television contracts and not as concerned with the education and welfare of its student athletes.

In 1969, the first national collegiate basketball tournament, a single-elimination, invitational tournament, was held in West Chester, Pennsylvania. The tournament featured 16 teams from around the country. West Chester State defeated Western Carolina in the championship game, played by six-player rules. Many colleges were experimenting with five-player rules, but tournament officials felt the national championship should be played by the rules still officially on the books.

The following year, Northeastern University's coach, Jeanne Rowlands, organized and hosted the National Invitational Tournament, the last ever played by six-player rules. Cal State-Fullerton, coached by Billie Jean Moore, traveled coast to coast to defeat West Chester State in the title game. The 1971 invitational tournament, the first under five-player rules, was at Western Carolina University. Mississippi College for Women won over West Chester State.

By 1971, every state high school association had officially switched to the five-player game except

Tara VanDerveer

In the stands watching the 1972 AIAW tournament was a young woman named Tara VanDerveer. She had driven with four college friends from Albany, New York, to Illinois to see the AIAW championship in Normal.

VanDerveer wanted a chance to play high-caliber basketball. She had grown up in the 1960s in Niagara Falls, where there was no high school girls basketball team. She tried out for the cheerleading squad instead but didn't make it. She'd had to borrow another girl's gym suit, and when all the snaps popped open the first time she spread her arms to do a cheer, she knew she was doomed.

VanDerveer was delighted that the state college in Albany had a women's basketball program. But many of the players on the team had as little playing experience as she did. After they got clobbered by Queens in a late-season game her freshman year, VanDerveer decided to transfer to a school where she could improve and would have a chance of winning.

VanDerveer spent most of the four days of the 1972 AIAW tournament in the stands taking notes on the 16 teams she watched. She liked Indiana because the coach, a graduate assistant, seemed to have a good grasp of the game and also played most of her young players for at least a few minutes of each game. VanDerveer also was excited about the possibility of watching the Indiana men's team, coached by legendary Bobby Knight. After she transferred to Indiana, she scheduled her classes so that she would be free during the men's practice time. Almost every day, she sneaked into the practices and sat high in the bleachers, taking notes on the way Knight coached.

"Just hearing the same things from Knight over and over, day after day, and watching, watching, watching, my brain formed patterns for how the game should be played," she recalled in her 1993 book *Shooting from the Outside.*

VanDerveer went on to coach at Stanford, leading the women's team to the national championship in 1990 and 1992. She also coached the 1996 U. S. Olympic team, which won a gold medal.

*In 1970, 50.6
percent of
high school
girls in Iowa
played sports
as opposed to
less than half
that in the rest
of the country.*

Iowa and Oklahoma. At that time, girls basketball was outdrawing boys basketball and funding many other girls sports programs in Iowa. School officials, parents, and even players feared that if girls basketball lost its distinctiveness, it would compete more directly with boys for fans and support and lose its popularity. Some also feared that many girls, particularly those who weren't as talented as others, couldn't play a full-court game. They noted proudly that 50.6 percent of high school girls in Iowa played sports in 1970 as opposed to less than half that in the rest of the country.

"Our Iowa game provides an extra player with an opportunity to play," said Ruth Ashton Johnson, who was one of two women on the Iowa Girls' High School Athletic Union Board of Directors in the mid-1970s. Johnson grew up in Iowa City, one of the cities where girls weren't allowed to play basketball, even in Iowa. She loved the game anyway.

"It [six-on-six] gives our girls a game which is both different and unique," Johnson said in 1975. "I love the six-player game. . . . Iowa has proved it's the best by test."

Everywhere else, though, girls had few regrets over the switch to the five-player game even if it did take some adjustment. Holly Warlick grew up playing six-on-six in high school in Knoxville, Tennessee. At the University of Tennessee in the mid-1970s, she had to learn to control her newfound freedom as a point guard.

"At first I was a hyper player with no control over my speed or my talent," she recalled in 1991. "All the shots I missed were layups, thrown with such speed and force that they practically banked back to half-court."

Warlick became an all-American. She broke the school's record for assists and steals and became the first player of the five-player era to have her jersey retired at Tennessee. She and other girls of her era learned to enjoy steals, rebounds, fast breaks, and assists as much as making a basket or blocking a shot. It didn't take long for girls to get into the flow of the full-court game.

In the early 1970s, college athletic departments typically spent only about 1 percent of their budget on women's sports. There were no athletic scholarships. The bigger schools weren't spending any more money on women's athletics than small colleges were. Any college coach had an equal chance of developing a winning team simply by finding the right combination of players.

When Lucille Kyvallos took over the fledgling women's basketball program at Queens College in New York in the early 1970s, she had her pick of inner-city girls from Queens, Brooklyn, or the Bronx. Similarly, when Cathy Rush began coaching the Mighty Macs of Immaculata College, she had her pick of the girls who grew up playing Catholic Youth Organization league ball in and around Philadelphia.

Kyvallos had grown up in Queens, the daughter of factory-working parents. She played basketball in a boys intramural league in junior high. Once she reached high school, she and some girlfriends formed a team of their own called the Rustics and entered the Police Athletic League. The Rustics won City Championships during Kyvallos's playing days, and she often won most valuable player trophies.

Kyvallos earned a degree in physical education at Springfield College in Springfield, Massachusetts. After graduation in 1955, Kyvallos played semi-pro ball for the New York Cover Girls, a team of women who, like the Red Heads, traveled around and challenged local men's teams to games.

Kyvallos took over the laid-back basketball program at Queens in 1968. Kyvallos decided to find women who, like her, had natural physical ability and had honed their skills on the playgrounds of New York. While other colleges were playing zone defense, she taught her team to play man-to-man defense. "That first season we won 10 out of 12 games," she recalled. "But more importantly, the women were learning the discipline necessary to become committed athletes."

For the 1971–72 season, Kyvallos assembled a group of players that held the opposing teams to 37

Cathy Rush, Immaculata coach

points while averaging 72 points themselves. Queens was selected to compete in the national tournament, which that year was held at Illinois State University. For the first time, the teams competing in the 1972 national tournament were chosen according to a regional qualifying structure that broke the country into 16 regions. The top team from each region, based on regular-season and regional tournament play, went to the national tournament.

Among the participants in the newly restructured tournament was Immaculata College. Players for the small, all-women, Catholic school looked demure in their round-collared blouses and pleated tunics but played an aggressive, fast-breaking game and tough, pressure defense. Theresa Shank was emblematic of them.

Shank grew up in Springfield, Pennsylvania, and starred for Cardinal O'Hara High School, leading it to Philadelphia CYO and citywide championships three years in a row. Shank, 5-foot-11 and 156 pounds, was quick and agile with a soft shooting touch and a sixth sense about the direction in which a missed shot would bounce off the rim.

Coach Rush's two-hour practices, consisting of 90 percent drills and wind sprints and very little scrimmaging, gave Immaculata the edge over most opponents when it came to conditioning. Immaculata also had an ardent cheering section—the nuns, called the Servants of the Immaculate Heart of Mary, who taught the students and lived on campus. With Shank scoring points and pulling down rebounds and the nuns banging on buckets, Immaculata defeated West Chester, 52–48, for the 1972 national championship.

By the beginning of the 1972–73 school year, campuses were buzzing about Title IX, the new federal law that had been passed the previous summer. Title IX made it illegal for any school receiving federal funding to discriminate against students on the basis of sex. Compliance was required by 1978.

Meanwhile, after the 1972 Olympics in Munich, the International Olympic Organizing Committee decided to include women's basketball in the next

Olympic Games, in Montreal in 1976. The AAU had selected players and overseen U. S. participation in international competition since 1953, but the Amateur Basketball Association of America took over as the governing body of U. S. international competition. From then on, teams and coaches for the Pan American Games, the World Championships, and the Olympics would come mainly from colleges.

In the meantime, the Association of Intercollegiate Athletics for Women decided to make the 1973 national tournament a four-day affair, betting that Queens and Immaculata would make it to the late rounds of the tournament and draw enough interest to pay expenses. Officials guessed right. Queens, led by 5-foot-11 freshman Gail Marquis, defeated a much taller team from the University of California at Riverside in the quarter-finals to advance to the final eight teams. Queens then defeated Stephen F. Austin State University in overtime and, later that day, defeated Indiana University to reach the finals against Immaculata. The Mighty Macs had defeated Southern Connecticut State College on a last-second tip-in shot by Shank to make it to the final.

Some 3,000 fans packed the gym for the championship. Reporters from *The New York Times, Newsday,* and *Sports Illustrated* were there to cover the event. Shank, who scored 104 points in four tournament games, led Immaculata to a 59–52 victory. "I hate those sprints Mrs. Rush has us run," Shank told reporters after the game, "but they make a tournament like this easy." The tournament earned a profit of $4,631.

Title IX mandated that if colleges had athletic scholarships for men, they had to offer scholarships to women too. By 1974, colleges began offering scholarships to female athletes, although the number and amounts of scholarships for women were still a pittance compared to those offered to men.

Out in Southern California, a young multi-sport star had been making headlines since elementary school. Ann Meyers, the sixth child in a family of

"I hate those sprints Mrs. Rush has us run, but they make a tournament like this easy."

11, seemed to have a promising future as a high jumper, but she wanted to follow in her older brother Dave's footsteps and play college basketball. Meyers was well known among college basketball coaches since she had made the U. S. national team while still in high school. UCLA coach Billie Jean Moore feared Meyers would go somewhere else if UCLA did not offer her a full scholarship. Thus, Meyers became the first female athlete to receive a full, four-year athletic scholarship to UCLA. She also became an all-American in her very first season.

Meyers's scholarship marked the beginning of the end of small-college dominance in women's intercollegiate basketball, but the smaller, more established schools continued to shine in tournament play through the mid-1970s. On February 22, 1975, 12,000 people saw Immaculata defeat Queens, 65–61, in the first women's intercollegiate basketball game ever at Madison Square Garden. The event was such a success that college officials continued to schedule games in large arenas. That year, the Eastman Kodak Company began sponsoring an all-America team, chosen by coaches from around the country. The fact that Kodak, a major U. S. corporation, would spend $3,000 to lend its name to the women's game, spurred other companies, such as Avon, New Balance, and adidas, to ride the wave of growing popularity of women's sports.

The 1974–75 college season also saw women's basketball get its first national exposure on a major television network. On January 27, 1975, a game between the University of Maryland and Immaculata was televised. The 1975 AIAW championship between Delta State and Immaculata (won by Delta State, 90–81) also was televised nationally, though on a delayed basis.

Delta State University was led by 6-foot-3 sophomore center Lusia Harris. Harris was the seventh of nine children in a poor farm family from Minter City, Mississippi. In the fall of 1973, Harris planned to enter Alcorn A&M, a black college without a basketball team. But Delta State coach Margaret Wade had other ideas. Wade had starred at Delta State

back in the 1920s. She had been coaching high school basketball for more than 20 years before she returned to Delta State in 1973. Delta State offered no athletic scholarships yet, but Wade found Harris an academic scholarship and a work-study job in the admissions office.

Harris made Delta State an instant winner. The team went 16–2 in 1973–74, her first year. In 1975–76, Harris led Delta State to an undefeated season and the national championship. Harris was named to the first Kodak All-America team. In the course of her career, she would average 26 points and 14.5 rebounds a game.

"Things sure were different then," Harris recalled in 1996. "There weren't very many tall girls, and the game was not nearly as fast. . . . But I'm proud of what we accomplished back then. I feel I helped pave the way."

Queens College and Immaculata College squared off in front of 12,000 people at Madison Square Garden in 1975.

9

OLYMPIAN PROMISE; PROFESSIONAL FAILURE

When the United States Olympic Committee held tryouts for the first U. S. women's Olympic basketball team, 250 young women showed up. Two female college coaches, Billie Jean Moore and Sue Gunter, would be selecting the best high school, college, and post-college players in an effort to upset the Soviet Union, which hadn't lost an international tournament game since 1958.

Among the Olympic hopefuls was Ann Meyers, the All-American from UCLA who had already participated in the 1975 World Championship games in Colombia and the Pan American Games in Mexico City. Meyers was by no means the only experienced player there.

Lusia Harris, the 6-foot-3 center from Delta State, also played in the 1975 Pan Am Games in Mexico City. International play was rougher and more physical than many U. S. college players were used to, but Harris would not be intimidated.

Opposite page: Nancy Lieberman's dazzling passes made her a force in women's basketball.

Nancy Lieberman

Pat Head, the coach of Tennessee since 1974, was a long shot. She had injured her anterior cruciate ligament during her senior year in college. Surgery left her with a 12-inch scar along the inside of her knee. She'd gained more than 20 pounds since the injury and lost a lot of mobility. Head sat the bench on the 1975 Pan American team, and Moore told her she didn't stand much of a chance of making the Olympic team. But Head worked out for six hours a day, gave up red meat, and lost weight. She made the team and became a starter and co-captain.

The player attracting the most media attention was a 5-foot-10 redhead from Brooklyn, New York, named Nancy Lieberman. In 1975, Lieberman was a 17-year-old high school senior who developed her no-look passes and uncanny shooting eye on the playgrounds of the city. While she was a natural point guard because of her quickness and passing skills, Lieberman had a cockiness that made her believe she could throw elbows and get rebounds even against taller, bigger opponents.

"You don't find many guards who will rebound the way she does," said Marianne Stanley, who recruited Lieberman out of high school in 1976. "I don't think I've seen too many people who have her confidence. You can't teach that. . . . She probably came out of the womb swinging."

The U. S. team won a pre-Olympic qualifying tournament in Ontario, but its overall lack of preparation became apparent at the Montreal Games. The Americans lost to Japan, 84–71, but then defeated Bulgaria the next day, 95–79. The United States also beat Canada, 89–75. But then came the powerful Soviets.

Lusia Harris managed to score 18 points against the Soviets, but she could do nothing to stop 7-foot, 280-pound Uljana Semjonova. A lefthander with a soft touch around the basket, Semjonova scored 32 points even though she played little more than a half, as the Soviets defeated the U. S. team, 112–77.

"The Soviet strategy was simple," wrote *The New York Times* the next day. "Miss Semjonova simply stationed herself like a pillar under the basket . . .

and grabbed rebounds as if she were picking cherries in the Ukraine. Then, as her teammates worked the ball down court, she would lumber behind them . . . and tower beneath her own basket for an almost certain score. The United States players, scrappy but less practiced than their foes, leaped about her like puppies yelping for their lunchtime snack."

Because this first Olympics was a round-robin tournament, the U. S. team still had a chance for the silver medal if it could win its last game against Czechoslovakia. That game was tied at halftime, but the U. S. team went on a 15-point run in the second half that sealed the victory. Harris, no doubt relieved to be rid of the towering presence of Semjonova, led all scorers with 17 points. Bulgaria also had a 3–2 record but one of those losses was to the U. S. team, so the Americans were awarded the silver medal.

Back home, sports opportunities for high school girls had increased tremendously. Many states that had abandoned postseason tournaments in the 1930s or '40s re-instituted them. Before 1973, only eight states had state high school basketball tournaments for girls. By 1977, all but New York held sanctioned state tournaments. Because of Title IX, girls were getting more gym time, better uniforms, and earning varsity letters for their participation, just like the boys. Coaches at the high school level were being paid more equitably.

Lusia Harris's Delta State won its third straight AIAW championship in 1977, defeating Louisiana State University, 68–55, in front of 4,500 fans at the University of Minnesota in Minneapolis. The New Orleans Jazz of the National Basketball Association drafted Harris in the seventh round but she did not sign a contract or go to training camp. Harris was the second woman to be drafted by an NBA team. The San Francisco Warriors had drafted Denise Long as their 13th pick in 1969. She didn't play for them, but she did work out with them. Long had a storybook career for Iowa's Union-Whitten High School, scoring more than 6,000 points over the

Lusia Harris

A History of Basketball for Girls and Women

course of her four-year career, including an 111-point game and a 64-point game in the 1968 state championship game, which Union-Whitten won in overtime.

In 1978, in an effort to generate more publicity and exposure, the AIAW decided to expand the college tournament to 32 teams that would play each other at four satellite sites. The four regional winners would then advance to the first "Final Four" in women's basketball at UCLA. The strategy generated national TV coverage, an audience of 9,500 at the final, and $37,000 in profits. The semifinal game between Meyers's UCLA and Carol Blazejowski's Montclair State gave fans a chance to see two of the best players in women's basketball. Blazejowski had become a scoring whiz at Montclair State. She set a record for most points in a single game at Madison Square Garden (52) and had the highest points per game average of any college player (31.7).

The fact that UCLA won that game and went on to capture the championship by defeating the University of Maryland heralded the end of small-college dominance in women's basketball. A freshman on that UCLA team, Denise Curry, would be a four-year star just like Meyers had been, breaking Meyers's scoring records by her senior year. Big schools were luring the most talented players, like Curry, away from small schools such as Delta State and Immaculata.

In the late 1970s, black women began speaking up about the not-so-subtle racism they saw in women's college basketball. In 1979, Vivian Stringer, who coached the all-black Cheyney State team, objected to the exclusion of black teams from the Hanes All-America Classic and the small number of blacks on ABAUSA teams, which represented the United States in international competition. Lusia Harris was the only black player to join white players as a celebrity. Even Lynette Woodard—the NCAA's all-time leading scorer with 3,649 points and a Kodak All-American four years, from 1978 to 1981, at the University of Kansas—got relatively little attention during her career.

Lynette Woodard

There were other concerns about girls basketball, too. Some high school players and their parents considered a college team's reputation as either homosexual or straight as they sorted through scholarship offers. At least one college coach, Rene Portland of Penn State, who had played with Theresa Shank and Marianne Stanley at Immaculata, admitted to telling her basketball recruits that lesbians were not welcome on her team.

It's impossible to quantify homophobia's impact on the growth of basketball in the 1970s. As in earlier times, girls with a passion for basketball weren't deterred from playing, but girls with marginal talent or those who had talent in both basketball and a sport considered more feminine, such as gymnastics, might have given up basketball to avoid being stereotyped.

Coaches, too, were affected by stereotypes. More and more men began coaching girls and women's teams in the 1970s. Money and opportunity were the primary reasons for the increase, but some administrators were also uncomfortable with female coaches who did not exhibit what they considered a feminine image.

"The lesbian issue is a very real employment issue," said Donna Lopiano, the executive director of the Women's Sports Foundation. "Whenever a woman departs from a predominantly male idea of what a woman should be, there is discrimination against her."

Until 1978, women who wanted to make a living playing basketball had to go overseas. There were many teams to choose from in such countries as Ireland, France, Italy, Spain, and Japan. As in the old AAU industrial leagues, corporations sponsored the women's teams.

The presence of Americans on a team sparked interest among fans and the local media, but often the U. S. players were not treated like royalty. In the worst cases, some players were sexually harassed by male coaches or fans. More often, the American players lived an isolated existence in a country where they didn't know the language.

"It was really hard for me," recalled Lynette Woodard of her experience on an Italian team. "It was the first time I had been away from home and I didn't know the language. But I had to stay because I gave my word."

Bill Byrne, previously the director of player personnel for a short-lived World Football League team in Chicago, led the effort to create a U. S. women's professional basketball league. Byrne's three-year business plan was to capitalize on the growing interest in women's college basketball and then use the attention surrounding the 1980 Olympics to generate even more excitement for his new league.

Byrne and his business group received 750 applications for franchises in the Women's Professional Basketball League (WBL). They chose eight franchises—Iowa, New Jersey, Milwaukee, Chicago, Minnesota, Ohio, New York, and Houston—charging them each $50,000 to be part of the historic 1978–79 season. The franchise holders selected 80 of the top college seniors and free agents at the first WBL player draft on July 18, 1978. Salaries in the league varied from team to team. Some players earned $100 a game for a 36-game season. The Chicago Hustle paid players $8,000 to $12,000 a year.

Houston drafted Lusia Harris, but she decided not to give up her position as an admissions counselor at Delta State for the paltry sum she would earn in the WBL. Lieberman was still in college. Blazejowski and Meyers, who had graduated in 1978, decided to remain amateurs so that they could compete in the 1980 Olympics.

Molly Bolin, the first woman to sign with the WBL, had a one-year contract with Iowa that called for her to earn $6,000. Bolin had been an amazing long-range jump shooter in the Iowa six-on-six high school game, scoring 80 points in one game and 70 in another. She scored 16 points a game in her rookie WBL season, despite having had no experience in the five-player game. Bolin's blonde hair, blue eyes, and slender figure made her a favorite with male sportswriters.

Molly Bolin

"People always warned me about exploitation," she said after she had posed for a promotional poster in a tank top and tight-fitting shorts in 1980. "But it's all about putting people in the seats, isn't it? You don't have to look like a man, act like one, or play like one in this game. . . . If you really want to make it when you're new, you've got to grab everything you've got and go with it."

The Chicago Hustle, the Iowa Cornets, and the Houston Angels were the three most successful teams at the box office and on the court in the first year. Close to 6,000 fans in Houston watched the Angels come from behind to defeat the Iowa Cornets, 111–104, for the first WBL championship. Every team lost money that first year, but hopes were high for the second season. League officials hoped to pick up more sponsors and convince one of the television networks to broadcast games on a regular basis.

Meanwhile, intercollegiate basketball continued to grow. In 1979, an Immaculata grad, Marianne Stanley, became the first woman to win national championships as a player and then a coach when her team, Old Dominion, defeated Louisiana Tech, once again in front of a national television audience. The matchup, which showcased Lieberman's flamboyant playing style as well as the flashy coaching style and outspoken personality of Tech's Sonja Hogg, delighted the media. The game also featured two 6-foot-5 players pitted against each other: ODU's Inge Nissen and Tech's Elinore Griffin.

Meyers's alma mater, UCLA, came in third in 1979, but the big news in Los Angeles that spring was the NBA draft. The Indiana Pacers had selected Meyers and signed her to a $50,000 contract. Meyers spent three days in tryouts with the Pacers but did not make the team.

Meyers and Blazejowski played on the U. S. national team in the Pan American Games and the World Championships in the summer of 1979. Meyers was the first woman ever to carry the U. S. flag during the opening ceremony of the Pan Am Games. With Meyers and "Blaze" leading the scoring, the U. S. team defeated the Soviet Union for the

Olympian Promise; Professional Failure

Ann Meyers

first time since 1959 and won the gold medal in the World Championships. They came in second to the Soviets at the Pan Am Games.

After the Pan Am Games, Meyers decided to give up her amateur status to sign with the WBL, which expanded in its second year from eight to 14 teams. The Dayton, Ohio, team moved west and became the St. Louis Streak. The new teams included the Dallas Diamonds, the San Francisco Pioneers, the California Dream, the New Orleans Pride, the Philadelphia Fox, and the Washington, D. C., Metros. The Pioneers were co-owned by television stars Mike Connors of *Mannix* fame and Alan Alda of *M*A*S*H*.

San Francisco and Dallas proved to be popular, well-run franchises, but the expansion strained the finances of all the teams because of the increased travel and game expenses. Players often went without meal money and, sometimes, their paychecks. Teams traveled by bus to some games, and players ate their meals at truckstops or diners. Without money, teams couldn't publicize games. When newspapers began writing negative stories about poor attendance and the players' plight, sponsors and advertisers stayed away from the league.

The New York Stars, led by Queens graduate Althea Gywnn, won the second league championship. The Iowa Cornets were again the runners-up. But a few weeks later, the Stars and Cornets, along with the Milwaukee Does, the Houston Angels, and the teams in Philadelphia and Washington, D. C., all folded because they couldn't pay their players. The California Dreams moved to Nebraska and became the Wranglers. The league's remaining owners fired founder Bill Byrne.

Adding more controversy to the troubled league, some of the league's black players accused the WBL's owners of racism. While there were plenty of blacks on the eight teams that started the league, the big names—Bolin and Meyers—were white. In an *Ebony* magazine article in 1980, black players spoke out about the racism of the league. "This is a white girls' league," said one black player, who didn't want to be named. "They [the owners] feel that because pro women's basketball is a new product, they can't afford to have it dominated by black girls."

Just before the start of the league's third season. Meyers refused to report to the New Jersey Gems for training camp because the team hadn't paid her full salary. Meyers had signed a $130,000, three-year contract, but the team hadn't issued her a paycheck since May 1980. The team finally paid her most of what she was owed in October, but she decided to hold out for the rest and the team tried to trade her. No other team picked up her contract because it was so much more than what other players were being paid. "I've learned a lot in the last two years," said Meyers in a 1980 *Women's Sports* article. "Sports is a business. . . . If they can use you, fine, and once they can't, that's it."

In the college game, Nancy Lieberman had once again led Old Dominion to the national championship in 1980. ODU defeated Pat Head's University of Tennessee in front of a national TV audience, 68–53. For the second year in a row, Lieberman won the Wade trophy, which honored Margaret Wade, the pioneer coach from Delta State.

The United States had boycotted the 1980 Olympics in Moscow to protest the Soviet Union's invasion of Afghanistan, so women's basketball did not get the exposure league officials had hoped for from the Olympic Games. But Lieberman and Carol Blazejowski would be joining the league and attracting publicity. Despite the problems of expansion the year before, the WBL voted to add another team for 1980–81, bringing the total number of teams to nine.

Adding Lieberman in Dallas and Blazejowski to the New Jersey Gems did indeed boost attendance and media coverage of the whole league. But in 1981, financial problems once again dominated the headlines. The league's newest entry, the New England Gulls, was a glaring example of how badly managed the league was.

The Gulls owner, an ex-school teacher and a liquor store owner from Lynn, Massachusetts,

Nancy Lieberman celebrates Old Dominion's second national championship, in 1980.

"The reason
we are quitting
is because we
can't go on.
We can't pay
our rents, we
can't buy
food. We've
been taken
advantage of
because we
love this game
so much."

named Joseph Reither, had declared bankruptcy in 1976. League officials knew about it when they awarded him a franchise in 1980. But, as new commissioner Sherwin Fischer explained, the board of directors was impressed with Reither's ability to assemble an organization, find an arena to play in, and hire a respected coach (former Boston Celtic Jim Loscutoff) to lead the team. And the league needed a quick replacement on the schedule for Tampa Bay, Florida, which had backed out at the last minute.

Reither seemed flush with cash. He drove a fancy Cadillac and carried around a huge wad of cash. During training camp, he put the players up at the Holiday Inn and bought them room service. After one preseason game, he treated the players at an upscale restaurant. He gave each of the players a $100 bill when they left for Christmas break.

But by then, players' paychecks had already started bouncing. Unable to buy groceries, some players sneaked into the nearby Merrimack College cafeteria for breakfast. Two players who had been cut from the team in December shared their food stamps with the rest of the team. In mid-January, the players staged a walkout before a game against San Francisco in Portland, Maine, demanding to be paid. Reither told the players they could have the gate receipts if they agreed to play. But he asked them to sign statements releasing him from breach of contract claims. And he told them they would have to pay the officials who worked the game. Reither hadn't spent any money on advertising or pregame promotion. There were only 200 or so people in the stands waiting for the game to start. Arena managers told the players they'd probably end up owing the arena money, even before they paid the referees. The players realized they had no choice but to get back on the team bus, pack up their bags, and give up their dreams.

"The reason we are quitting is because we can't go on. We can't pay our rents, we can't buy food. We've been taken advantage of because we love this game so much," said team captain Chris Critelli, who was leading the Gulls in scoring that season.

"Women's basketball is a concept whose time has come," Scott Lang, an agent who represented many WBL players, said in 1981. "But it can't last with the cast of characters it has had running it."

The league limped through the final months of its third season. The Nebraska Wranglers held Nancy Lieberman to 12 points, 14 below her average, to win the 1980–81 championship over Dallas, 99–90. Teams had lost an average of $350,000 each that third year. St. Louis canceled its last road trip for lack of funds. Dave Almstead, owner of the Diamonds, was named interim commissioner that spring after Fischer resigned. Almstead called three meetings of owners that summer and no one showed up. He sent out a press release announcing that the WBL was officially dead.

The league's players were disappointed and disillusioned. After the WBL folded, Bolin stayed in San Francisco and worked as a roofer. "I'm pretty lost," she said in 1981. "I promoted my ass off to make this work. I don't know anyone who wasn't burned."

Many other WBL players either embarked on coaching careers or continued to play overseas. Ann Meyers was luckier. She already had been sidelined by her contract dispute. To keep busy, she'd signed on to appear on television specials that showcased male and female athletes competing in various sports. By the mid-1980s, Meyers began broadcasting basketball games.

Lieberman became tennis star Martina Navratilova's trainer. She taught the erratic and undisciplined Navratilova the value of strength training and being in top physical shape. The training helped Navratilova's career take off and ushered in a new era of strength and fitness to a sport that had not been known for its physicality.

Lieberman also began a career broadcasting Old Dominion games and providing analysis on telecasts of NCAA playoff games. It would be another five years before Lieberman got the chance to shine on the basketball court again.

10

Growing Pains in the '80s

With basketball leading the way, the number of girls competing in high school sports increased from 300,000 in 1970 to 2 million by 1980. The bigger pool of talented players available to colleges enabled those programs to expand as well. In 1981, 880 colleges fielded basketball teams, and 529 of them offered a total of $4.8 million in full or partial scholarships to 6,000 women.

The 1981 Division I championship was held at the University of Oregon, and Louisiana Tech defeated the Lady Vols, 79–59, to capture its first national title. NBC-TV broadcast the final game. Its four-year contract to televise the Division I, II, and III tournaments yielded nearly $1 million in revenue for the AIAW.

But along with the financial boost, the AIAW got a fight. The NCAA had previously had little interest in women's sports, but its governing board of male athletic directors decided in late 1981 to offer its own women's basketball tournaments the following year. Title IX had prompted many colleges to merge

Opposite page: Cheryl Miller drives against an overmatched defender.

"People who say just trust the NCAA, they'll do what's right for women, are totally naive. Their track record in women's athletics is dismal."

their men's and women's intercollegiate athletic programs to save money. The men's athletic director was usually promoted to run the merged department, and the women's director often moved to a secondary position. Many male athletic directors didn't want women's programs governed by a separate structure like the AIAW, which some considered more restrictive in terms of scholarships, academic requirements, and recruiting. The NCAA also began offering incentives, such as free travel to NCAA tournament games, to switch from the AIAW to the NCAA. The simplicity of having only one set of rules and the incentives convinced 240 college athletic directors to abandon the AIAW and join the NCAA in early 1982.

The AIAW did not give up without a fight. The organization filed an antitrust lawsuit against the NCAA, charging that the NCAA did not have women's best interests at heart. They cited the NCAA's public opposition to passage of Title IX legislation back in the early 1970s. "People who say just trust the NCAA, they'll do what's right for women are totally naive," said Christine Grant, athletic director at the University of Iowa in 1981. "Their track record in women's athletics is dismal."

Seventeen of the top 20 women's basketball teams chose to compete in the NCAA's inaugural postseason tournament in 1982, held at Old Dominion in Norfolk, Virginia. Louisiana Tech won the championship by defeating Cheyney State, 76–62. Close to 10,000 fans watched the final game, which CBS-TV broadcast and which earned a 7.3 rating for its share of the TV audience.

That same weekend, the AIAW held its 1982 tournament at the University of Pennsylvania. Rutgers, coached by former Immaculata star Theresa Shank Grentz, defeated Jody Conradt's University of Texas. NBC-TV had broken its contract with the AIAW, fearing the competition with the NCAA, so the game was not televised. Attendance was poor, and the tournament lost $8,800.

That was the AIAW's final tournament. Hundreds more schools defected, and when only 95 of its 759 members said they would send delegates to the AIAW's upcoming conference in June 1982, the organization disbanded, and its antitrust suit was dismissed.

The problems AIAW officials had predicted did materialize but not for women's basketball. A 1987 study showed that the NCAA was holding fewer national championships in fewer sports than the AIAW had in 1981. But the NCAA had realized that women's basketball could be a moneymaker. In 1983, the NCAA used its clout to gain more television exposure for women's basketball. For the first time, the all-sports cable network ESPN televised tournament games before the championship. CBS-TV again carried the final game.

Viewers glimpsed the future of women's basketball in that title game. Freshman Cheryl Miller and the University of Southern California challenged defending national champion Louisiana Tech in front of 7,387 fans. As a high school senior, Miller had been the most sought-after basketball player in the country. At 6-foot-2, she could dunk the ball as easily as any male. She scored 105 points in one high school game, and she led her team, Riverside Poly High School, to 84 straight wins and two state championships.

USC trailed Louisiana Tech at halftime 37–26, thanks to Janice Braxton's 17 first-half points. Coach Linda Sharp decided at halftime that USC would have to come out pressing full-court in the second half if the Trojans were going to get back into the game—even though USC hadn't pressed a team all year. "I thought she had flipped," recalled Miller. "Everyone on our team knew that our third string could beat our press and now we were going to try it against the two-time defending national champs?"

But the press worked. It forced Louisiana into turnovers and got USC's emotional players fired up on offense. Miller dove for loose balls, took charges, and made steals to lead the comeback. Her 27 points were a record at the time. Her nine rebounds, four blocked shots, and four steals also helped seal the 69–67 victory. "It was the most incredible game I've ever been in," recalled Miller 12 years later on the

Lynne Lorenzen

In 1987, the six-player game was still going strong in Iowa. That year, the state crowned a new all-time scoring champion as Lynne Lorenzen finished her four-year career at Ventura High with 6,736 points, an amazing 60 points per game average.

Lorenzen was the daughter of Frances Billerbeck Lorenzen, one of the famous twins who led the 1952 Rhinebeck High School team to the state championship. Frances had three basketball-playing daughters. Lynne was the youngest. She and her sisters practiced in the hayloft of their barn after school. Lynne's older sisters made her get the rebounds for them when she was a second grader. By the time she was in seventh grade, she was challenging her mother to shoot-around games. "Mom beat me two out of three," recalled Lynne in a book about Iowa basketball.

Lynne was a four-year starter on the Ventura High varsity. Her freshman year, she scored 47 points per game. By her senior year, the whole state knew that she had a shot at the high school girls scoring record, which another Iowan, Denise Long, had set in 1969. Long, of Union-Whitten High, was a legend in Iowa. She and Jennette Olson of Everly High School scored 140 points between them in the 1968 state championship—the greatest shootout in girls basketball history. Union-Whitten beat Everly 113-107 in overtime. Long had ended her career in 1969 with 6,250 points.

Long's record had gone unnoticed outside of Iowa, but Lorenzen's quest to break it became national news. Reporters came from all over the country to the district tourney, when Lorenzen only needed a few points to break Long's record.

Lorenzen went on to play at Iowa State University where she had to learn how to play defense, develop the stamina for the full-court game, and adjust to being able to take more than two dribbles. Still, she's glad she played the six-player game.

"I'm all for the six-player game," she said in a 1989 *Sports Illustrated* article. "My high school had a senior class of 24 and you need a lot of good athletes to play five on five. We could not have done it. But I'd be a better player if I'd played five on five."

eve of her induction into the Naismith Memorial Basketball Hall of Fame. "It was Easter Sunday and we got our Easter gift."

In 1984, high school and college women began using a smaller, lighter basketball. The ball certainly made it easier for girls ages 8 to 12 to develop their skills, but predictions that it would improve play in high school and college didn't pan out. A study of college games that year proved that the ball made little difference in terms of total points, rebounds, steals, turnovers, fouls, or assists.

As girls basketball began receiving more attention nationwide, Iowans began to wonder if it made sense to have girls play by the six-player rules. Some argued that girls who graduated from high school in Iowa were at a disadvantage when competing for college scholarships because they had no experience with the full-court game. In 1984, three high school girls in Iowa sued the Iowa Girls High School Athletic Union under Title IX, charging that the six-on-six game limited their opportunities and was not equal to the five-player game.

Supporters of the status quo rushed to the game's defense. They pointed out that the girls' tournament made enough money to support 15 sports. The game also gave more girls the opportunity to play. Old-timers talked about tradition. Former players who had gone on to play in college said it wasn't that difficult to make the switch.

The Iowa athletic union decided to continue to sponsor the six-player tournament, but to avoid the lawsuit, officials also began holding a five-on-five tournament as well. High schools could compete in either tournament. Fewer than 100 schools, most of them city schools that had not even sponsored basketball for girls until the 1970s, opted for the five-player game. More than 450 schools, most of them in small communities, continued to compete in the six-player tournament.

In 1984, Miller and company again won the NCAA Division I national championship in front of a hometown crowd of 5,365 at UCLA. USC defeated Louisiana Tech, 62–57, in the semifinals. In the

Cheryl Miller

Teresa Edwards leaps for a rebound in a 1984 Olympic game.

finals, USC defeated Tennessee, 72–61. Once again, Miller was the Most Valuable Player, but now she was also the most visible symbol of how much women's basketball had changed. With a starting lineup that usually included at least four black players, USC had changed the public image of women's basketball. The stars that had been promoted just five years before had been mostly white women. The stars of the 1980s were black. And some, like Miller, were not afraid to speak their minds and strut their stuff.

"I played to the crowds. I was an entertainer," Miller said in 1995. "As long as you have passionate players who capture the attention of the audience, that's all women's basketball needs."

Some people didn't agree. San Diego State coach Ernest Riggins called Miller a "typical hot dog" after one game in which she continually wagged her finger, blew kisses to the crowd, and did cheerleader-type leaps after her baskets. He told *Sports Illustrated* that he had lost a lot of respect for her.

Nancy Lieberman, who was working as a color commentator on some TV broadcasts of women's games, came to Miller's defense. "The flamboyance is her bread and butter," said Lieberman. "I think Cheryl is the best thing that could have happened to the game."

Miller joined a 1984 U. S. Olympic team loaded with talent. The Soviet Union was boycotting the Games, which would be held in Los Angeles, in retaliation for the 1980 U. S. boycott. The Soviets were still the dominant team in international play, and their absence gave the U. S. team hope for the gold medal.

Tennessee coach Pat Head Summitt chose two of her Tennessee players—Lea Henry and Cindy Noble—along with Miller and Pamela McGee from USC, Lynette Woodard of Kansas, Kim Mulkey and Janice Lawrence of Louisiana Tech, Cathy Boswell of Illinois State, Denise Curry of UCLA, Carol Menken-Shaudt of Oregon State, and Teresa Edwards, a college sophomore at the University of Georgia, for the U. S. team.

Another obvious choice was Anne Donovan, a 1983 graduate of Old Dominion. Because of her 6-foot-8 frame and her jumping ability, she gave the U. S. team the inside threat it had so sorely lacked in 1976 against the Soviet Union. Donovan also had the speed to get out on the fast break and get back on defense in time to stop the other team's break. She had a good outside shot as well as a deadly hook shot.

The U. S. team easily disposed of Yugoslavia, Australia, Korea, and China in the opening round-robin competition. The Americans remained undefeated, capturing the gold medal in a lopsided game against Korea, 85–55. Miller led all scorers.

Right after the Olympics, Lynette Woodard became the first woman ever to wear the uniform of the Harlem Globetrotters. She had an older cousin who had played for the Globetrotters, and she had dreamed, as a kid, of wearing the Globetrotters' red, white, and blue. Woodard stayed with the Globetrotters for two years. She left when the team increased its already grueling exhibition schedule from six to nine months. Within a month of leaving the team in 1986, a team in Tokyo asked her to play. As women did in the old industrial leagues, she worked at the sponsor's company, a brokerage firm, by day and played basketball at night.

Nancy Lieberman, at 28, wasn't interested in playing overseas in 1986. But when the United States Basketball League, an all-male league of NBA hopefuls, drafted her, she jumped at the chance. Lieberman's time with the Springfield Fame of the USBL made her the first woman ever to play in a men's pro league. Serving as her own agent and promoter, Lieberman earned enough money from her salary, two instructional books, her endorsements, and two sporting goods stores to become the first millionaire in women's basketball.

Lieberman gave 270 interviews in her first three weeks with the team, and little girls wanting autographs mobbed her after games. The ball she used to score her first point and the jersey she wore are in the Basketball Hall of Fame. But she found herself mostly sitting on the bench, averaging one point

Lynette Woodard put on the red, white, and blue of the Harlem Globetrotters after helping to win the gold medal for the United States.

A History of Basketball for Girls and Women

Nancy Lieberman played for three professional leagues before joining the Washington Generals.

and one assist in less than 12 minutes a game. Lieberman still threw crowd-pleasing, no-look passes and shot the open jumper with ease, but her offensive skills and even her quickness didn't help when she found herself sandwiched between two 6-foot-8 male players setting bruising picks on her. Some women were critical of her for even playing.

"What does it mean if one out of every 2,000 women is good enough to play with men," said Heidi Wayment, a veteran of the European pro leagues, in an article in *Women's Sports and Fitness* magazine. "I'm glad for her but this makes it seem as if she's good because she can play with men, instead of just good."

In 1988, Lieberman left the USBL and joined the Washington Generals, the team that travels with and plays against the Harlem Globetrotters. As Woodard had, she found the exhibition tour exhausting, but she stuck with it. "I feel like I'm paving a big fat road," she said. "I've always wanted to be a leader, not a follower. There might be bigger and better players who come along and play in men's leagues, but I'll always be the first."

By 1988, women's college basketball had grown substantially. Athletic departments spent more on basketball and other women's sports to comply with Title IX. Many college coaches organized summer clinics for high school girls. High schools that previously had one coach to oversee both junior varsity and varsity teams hired assistant coaches. Junior high schools, which previously had offered only intramural sports for girls, began hiring coaches and scheduling games against other schools. And the AAU, which had lost its status as the Olympic training ground, began organizing leagues and tournaments for teams of girls age 12 and up.

All this activity expanded the pool of talented players for college basketball. From a field of 32 teams in 1984, the NCAA women's tournament expanded to 40 teams in 1988. In that four-year span, four different teams came out on top. In 1985, Old Dominion, coached by Marianne Stanley, won its first NCAA national title and third overall by defeating Georgia, 70–65. In 1986, Texas defeated USC 97–81 for its first championship. Tennessee defeated Louisiana Tech in the 1987 final, 66–44, to win its first title. And in 1988, Louisiana Tech won its second NCAA title and third overall by defeating Auburn, 56–54.

While Louisiana Tech had won the championship before, this was the first victory for Leon Barmore, the former Tech assistant coach who inherited the top job from Sonja Hogg in 1982 when he was 27 years old. It was also the first time a man had coached a women's team to the national championship since Harley Redin's Wayland Baptist teams and John Head's Nashville Business teams dominated in the 1950s and '60s.

The emergence of Barmore coincided with the emergence of many male coaches in women's college sports in the mid-1980s. In 1973, women were coaching 92 percent of all women's college teams. By 1987, the figure had dropped to 48 percent. In college basketball, the declines weren't quite as dramatic. According to one study, the percentage of women coaching women's basketball dropped from 80 to 61 percent between 1977 and 1985. High school athletics experienced a similar shift during the 1980s. In Colorado, for example, the percentage of women coaching girls high school teams dropped from 89 to 38 percent between 1971 and 1985.

One of the reasons for the change was experience. A school might prefer a man who had been coaching for 20 years over a woman with only five or six years of experience. Another reason might have been discrimination. Male athletic directors often were more comfortable hiring the friend of a friend. Some athletic directors hired men because they were afraid that women coaches would leave to raise children or that they were lesbians.

At the Olympic-level, women coaches still dominated. Kay Yow, the coach of North Carolina State, was chosen to coach the 1988 U. S. Olympic team. For the first time since 1976, both the United States and the Soviet Union would be competing. The Olympic Games moved from their traditional July

Cynthia Cooper threads her way to the basket despite the best efforts of the Soviet Union's 1988 squad.

and August time slot to mid-September because of the extreme heat and humidity of the host site—Seoul, Korea—in summer.

Yow had led the U. S. team to gold medals in the 1986 Goodwill Games and the world championships. She had surgery for breast cancer in 1987 but soon was preparing for Olympic tryouts. She chose her younger sister, Susan, as one of her assistants. The Yows' love of basketball blossomed during their childhood in North Carolina. Their mother had played for an industrial league team and their father, Virgil Yow, had coached Hanes Hosiery to three AAU championships in the 1950s.

Yow's team had just two returning veterans from the 1984 squad—Teresa Edwards and Anne Donovan. The star of the 1984 Games, Cheryl Miller, would not be making the trip to Korea because of a knee injury. Miller's former teammate at USC, Cynthia Cooper, would. Cooper had kept her skills sharp by playing in Spain since graduation. Suzie McConnell, a guard from Penn State, and Teresa Weatherspoon of Louisiana Tech made for a lightning-quick backcourt combination. Katrina McClain, Edwards's teammate at the University of Georgia, was an inside force who could hold her own against the Soviets. Cynthia Brown of Long Beach State, Vicky Bullett of Maryland, Mary Etheridge and Andrea Lloyd of Texas, Jennifer Gillom of Mississippi, and Bridget Gordon of Tennessee completed the team.

Uljana Semjonova, the 7-foot-2 Soviet center who had dominated international play since 1976, had retired in 1986. The U. S. team disposed of its other opponents in the preliminary rounds and then knocked off the Soviet team, 102–88, in the semifinals.

In the gold-medal game, the quickness of Weatherspoon and McConnell ran the Yugoslavs ragged. Yugoslavia had a 6-foot-7 center named Razija Mujanovic, but Edwards shot from the outside to lead the United States to a 77–70 victory. "For a long time, people have said this couldn't be done unless we had a certain player," Yow told reporters, "...but we have broadened our base of quality players."

The fact that the U. S. men lost to the Soviets further enhanced the women's game in the public's eye. NBC-TV only broadcast highlights of the women's games because of the time difference, but MTV, the music cable channel, invited the women's team to be on one of its shows to sing a rap song composed by Cooper.

Attendance soared at the 1989 and 1990 NCAA Division I championships. In 1989, the tournament expanded from 40 to 48 teams. Close to 10,000 fans at the Tacoma Dome in Washington saw Tennessee win its second national championship, 76–60, over Auburn. Bridget Gordon, an Olympic veteran, was named the Most Valuable Player.

In 1990, the women's Final Four outdrew the men's for the first time. The event was held in Knoxville, home of the defending champion Lady Vols. Tennessee lost in the regional tournament, but the crowds still came to Knoxville to watch Stanford, Auburn, Louisiana Tech, and Virginia play for the national championship. Jennifer Azzi, a Tennessean whom Stanford coach Tara VanDerveer had lured away, was the Most Valuable Player as Stanford defeated Auburn for the national title in front of 20,000 people.

But that very same March, the University of Oklahoma announced it was dropping women's basketball because the team was only attracting an average of 260 people to games. The news shocked Oklahoma students, parents, and state legislators. Protestors pointed out that half of all men's basketball programs across the country each lost $140,000 a year and that half of all football programs lost an average of $430,000 a year. Nobody was calling for those programs to be cut.

Five days later, after some students and parents threatened to sue, the school reinstated the basketball program. "But the fact remains that a large state university with a nationally prominent sports program tried to deny its female students the opportunity to play the most popular intercollegiate sport for females," wrote Kathryn Reith of the Women's Sports Foundation.

11

INTO THE SPOTLIGHT

After years of being paid less than male coaches, women's basketball coaches began fighting for pay equity. Sanya Tyler, the women's basketball coach at Howard University for 11 years, charged the university with discrimination in 1991. She said she had been denied the job of athletic director and was being paid considerably less than the men's basketball coach, despite her team's superior record. A jury awarded her $2.2 million, the first time a judgment of monetary damages had come from a lawsuit filed under Title IX. As a result, other women coaches began insisting on equal pay and some universities, including the University of Tennessee, began paying their women's coaches the same salary as their men's coaches.

But elsewhere, women were still second to men, as was glaringly obvious at the 1992 Olympics in Barcelona, Spain. For the first time, the Olympic Games were allowing professional basketball players to play. The U. S. men's team—with NBA superstars Michael Jordan, Magic Johnson, and Larry Bird—was dubbed the Dream Team. The U. S. women's team was going for its third straight gold medal but it had no nickname. The women stayed

Opposite page: The U. S. team took on Czechoslovakia in the 1992 Olympics while Magic Johnson, above, and the Dream Team dazzled the world.

111

A History of Basketball for Girls and Women

Cynthia Cooper returned to the U. S. squad for the 1992 Olympics.

with the U. S. athletes in the Olympic village, but the men were housed in luxury hotels.

"The U. S. had a Dream Team in 1984 and 1988—a dream team of women who won the gold medal," said Sonja Henning, a 1991 Stanford graduate who tried out for the Olympic team but didn't make it. "Those female athletes were not given the same kind of recognition. Maybe someday women will be treated as equals. Obviously that's not going to happen this summer."

But Theresa Shank Grentz, the U. S. women's coach, was more circumspect. "If the men were in the Olympic village, it would be a three-ring circus," she said in a *Sports Illustrated* article. "How would you provide security if Michael Jordan and Larry Bird were roommates?"

Grentz had the core of the team that won in Seoul returning, led by former Georgia teammates Teresa Edwards and Katrina McClain, and including Vicky Bullett, Cynthia Cooper, Suzie McConnell, and Teresa Weatherspoon. Because the Olympics allowed professionals, Cheryl Miller and Nancy Lieberman-Cline also tried out for spots on the team. Lieberman-Cline, 33 by then, didn't make the cut. Miller, 28, dropped out of contention with a knee injury before the cuts were made.

The United States expected China, with 6-foot-8 center Zheng Haixa, to be its stiffest competition. But the U. S. team had a surprisingly easy time against the Chinese, winning 93–67 to advance to the semifinals against the Unified Team, the former Soviet Union.

The U. S. team was so confident of at least making it to the gold-medal game that Grentz complained openly because NBC-TV was not going to broadcast that game in prime time. But the United States hadn't counted on the Unified Team being able to break its full-court press. The Unified Team coach, Yevgeny Gomelsky, was the younger brother of Aleksandr, the coach of the Soviet men's team in 1988, and the son of the woman who founded the first women's basketball team in St. Petersburg, Russia, in the 1920s.

The Unified Team easily broke the U. S. press by having a tall player receive the first pass inbounds and then pass it upcourt to one of the quick guards cutting the length of the court. At halftime, the U. S. team trailed, 54–43. Clarissa Davis and Carolyn Jones helped the Americans get the lead back briefly with 12 minutes to go, but McClain and Edwards shot poorly down the stretch, and McConnell made costly turnovers at point guard. The U. S. team lost, 79–73, and settled for the bronze medal, which it earned by defeating Cuba 88–74 in the consolation game. "I still feel like we're the best team here," a disappointed Edwards told reporters. "We just didn't prove it."

Into the Spotlight

Suzie McConnell swipes the ball during the U. S. team's victory over Cuba.

*Sheryl Swoopes led
Texas Tech to the 1993
NCAA championship.*

In 1992, Stanford University proved it was the best college team in the country, winning the NCAA Division I championship for the second time in three years. In 1993, two more new faces burst onto the national college stage as Texas Tech and Ohio State made it to the final game, played at Atlanta's Omni arena. Ohio State defeated Vivian Stringer's University of Iowa in an overtime thriller, 73–72, to make it to the finals. Texas Tech handily defeated Vanderbilt to advance.

Ohio State had a standout freshman in Katie Smith and a coach, Nancy Darsch, who had been an assistant under Pat Head Summitt during the 1980s. But Texas Tech had Sheryl Swoopes, a smooth shooting senior who had led Texas Tech to a 31–3 record and two straight Southwest Conference titles.

Swoopes was a shy, small-town Texas girl. She had accepted a scholarship to the University of Texas in Austin after leading her high school team to three state championships. But she was homesick in the city and, after three days, she quit and enrolled in a junior college a few miles from her home. After two years, she transferred to Texas Tech.

Swoopes's trademark shot was a jumper she could shoot from anywhere on the court. In the game against Ohio State, Darsch devised a special 2-3 zone just to contain Swoopes. But Swoopes shot 4-of-6 from three-point range to beat the zone. And even with Ohio State's Smith scoring 20 of her 28 points in the second half, Swoopes and Texas Tech prevailed. Swoopes wound up with 47 points, including 11 of 11 foul shots and an impossible shot from behind the backboard, to lead Texas Tech to a thrilling 84–82 victory. "You don't appreciate Swoopes until you have to stop her," said Darsch after the game. "She answered everything we tried."

The Ohio State–Texas Tech game was the highest rated women's final since the TV networks began televising games. Fourteen percent of Americans watching television that afternoon had the game on. The excitement generated by the game led to an almost instant sellout of tickets for the 1994 Final Four months before the season even started.

In high school basketball, 1993 was the year that Iowa finally gave up the six-player game. Money proved to be the deciding factor. By 1993, 134 schools were playing five-player ball and 275 still played six-on-six. The six-player tournaments were more popular, taking in an average of $800 more per game than the five-player tournament did. But officials with the Iowa Girls High School Athletic Union realized that by cutting one of the two girls basketball tournaments, 38 percent of its athletic budget could be used to fund other girls sports.

The High School Athletic Union planned on hosting the final two six-player tournaments in 1993 and 1994 but every conference in the state voted to switch to the five-player game for the 1993–94 season. So in March 1993, fans packed the arena in Des Moines one last time to see Hubbard-Radcliffe defeat Atlantic, 85–66, in the last six-player state championship game.

"It's been a romantic time, at least for the 39 years I've been here," said E. Wayne Cooley, the executive secretary of the Iowa Girls High School Athletic Union since the early 1950s. "The six-player tournament was the grande dame of the whole nation as far as women and girls basketball tournaments are concerned."

Oklahoma was the last outpost of six-on-six basketball in the country. Like Iowa, the state had a rich history of well-attended state tournaments and legendary teams. Oklahoma school officials voted in 1993 to switch to the five-player game. At that point, 110 schools played five on five and 369 still played six-on-six. The switch was made in the fall of 1995. Said Byng coach Bruce Plunk, "Six-on-six was great . . . But it was time to let it go."

If college basketball fans thought nothing could top Texas Tech's championship victory in 1993, the very next year proved otherwise. In 1994, the tournament expanded to 64 teams, just like the men's. Louisiana Tech and coach Leon Barmore advanced to their eighth Final Four since 1982 and defeated Alabama, 69–66. In the other semifinal, North Carolina easily handled Purdue, winning 89–74.

Louisiana Tech and North Carolina squared off for the 1994 NCAA title.

A History of Basketball for Girls and Women

Cheryl Miller returned to the University of Southern California in 1994 as the head coach.

In the title game, in front of a sellout crowd of 11,000 in Richmond, Virginia, Louisiana Tech held a two-point lead with just seconds to play. But UNC's Charlotte Smith, who led the Tar Heels in rebounds and was second in points, got the inbounds pass with a second still on the clock. Just before the buzzer sounded, she released a rainbow three-point shot that seemed to hang in the air for a minute before it swished through the net and gave North Carolina the victory, 60–59. It was the first time that the margin of victory in a women's title game was a single point.

The 1994 season also brought Cheryl Miller back into the limelight. The University of Southern California hired her after firing Marianne Stanley. Stanley, who had been coaching at USC since 1989, turned down a contract in 1993 that would have paid her $89,000 a year because the men's basketball coach at USC made $130,000 a year. Stanley sued USC for $8 million in back pay and damages. In response, the university hired Miller.

Miller's decision to take the job angered some of her female colleagues, who felt she had betrayed Stanley and the cause of pay equity. What made the women coaches even angrier was that Stanley, despite her credentials, was having trouble finding another job. "I applied for close to 100 jobs and had one interview," recalled Stanley in 1997. "My lawsuit was a lightning rod."

Players recruited by Stanley openly questioned Miller's loyalty to women's basketball, as well as her coaching credentials. One of those players was two-time all-American Lisa Leslie, recruited by Stanley from nearby Morningside High School in Los Angeles. The 6-foot-5 Leslie scored 30 points and grabbed 20 rebounds in her first game for USC her freshman year.

Miller told players they had no right to criticize her motives, only the results she got. In two years at USC, Miller proved she could coach, leading USC to a 44–14 record and the NCAA tournament both years. In early 1995, she was elected to the Naismith Memorial Basketball Hall of Fame.

In 1995, another new champion emerged to challenge the powerhouses of college basketball. In 1989, Geno Auriemma had taken the University of Connecticut to the NCAA tournament for the first time. Two years later, in 1991, the Lady Huskies made it to their first Final Four, where they lost a close game to Virginia in the semifinals.

That appearance was the recruiting tool Auriemma needed to lure top recruits away from the better-known schools such as Louisiana Tech, Tennessee, and Stanford. The biggest coup was keeping 6-foot-4 Rebecca Lobo of Southwick, Massachusetts, in New England. Lobo had averaged more than 30 points and 20 rebounds a game her senior year in high school. More than 100 colleges wanted Lobo to play for them. She chose Connecticut because it was only an hour away from home but also because Auriemma convinced her Connecticut could win a national championship. Also joining the team were Jennifer Rizzotti, a fiery point guard; Jamelle Elliot, a forward with a deft shooting touch, and Kara Wolters, a 6-foot-7 center.

By the time Lobo was a senior, the Lady Huskies were defeating most opponents by 20 points. They went into the 1995 NCAA tournament undefeated. Their biggest regular-season win was against Tennessee, which had been ranked number one.

By April's NCAA championship in Minneapolis, the Lady Huskies were 34–0 but no one expected them to beat Tennessee twice in one season. With Nikki McCray and Michelle Marciniak leading the way, the Lady Vols had beaten all their tournament foes by at least 18 points.

A record TV audience of 5.4 million and another 19,000 fans in Minneapolis, Minnesota, saw Tennessee come out strong against Connecticut. Tennessee led by six at halftime. With 12 minutes to go in the second half, Tennessee had increased its lead to nine. That's when Rebecca Lobo took over. She scored four quick baskets to bring the Lady Huskies to within one point. With two minutes to go, the score was tied. Then Rizzotti drove the length of the floor for a reverse layup to give the

Rebecca Lobo celebrates an undefeated season for the University of Connecticut.

Huskies the lead for good. Connecticut hung on to win, 70–64.

Thousands of people viewed women's basketball with new respect because of the Lady Huskies. In Hartford, 100,000 people stood along a parade route to greet the team upon its return. *The New York Times* put the Lady Huskies on its front page the next day. *Sports Illustrated* put Rizzotti on its cover beside the word "Perfect." Still, in terms of gaining respect, fans, and media support, the best for women's basketball was yet to come.

The 1996 Olympics were going to be held in the United States for the first time since 1984. Officials with USA Basketball did not want the world to see their women's team lose the gold medal in Atlanta, Georgia. USA Basketball and the NBA got companies such as Sears, Lifetime Television, State Farm Insurance, and Nike to contribute $6 million to finance a year-long training tour for the U. S. women's team in preparation for the 1996 Games.

Teresa Edwards was 32 in 1996—this would be her fourth Olympics—but she was still considered the top international player when she was among those picked in May 1995 for the U. S. national team. Sheryl Swoopes was another natural. After her stunning performance at the 1993 NCAA final, she had signed a contract with Nike that made her the first female basketball player to endorse a basketball shoe. The "Air Swoopes," like its "Air Jordan" men's counterpart, sold for more than $115 a pair.

Lisa Leslie, the USC star who had been the college player of the year in 1994, also made the team as its only pure center. Dawn Staley, the point guard who led Virginia to the NCAA finals against Tennessee in 1991, was another easy pick. She had been the college player of the year in 1991 and 1992.

Jennifer Azzi, who had been an alternate on the 1992 team, made the cut in 1996 along with her Stanford teammate, Katy Steding, a 6-foot forward. Ruthie Bolton-Holifield, a forward who starred for Auburn in the late 1980s and was earning six-figure salaries in Europe, and Rebecca Lobo, who had led Connecticut to the NCAA championship just a few

Teresa Edwards takes it to the hoop.

months earlier, also were chosen. Carla McGhee of Tennessee, who had missed most of her college career because of injuries she suffered in a devastating car crash in 1987, and Nikki McCray, newly graduated from Tennessee, rounded out the 11-member team. The official Olympic team wouldn't be chosen until the following May. Depending on their performances, these 11 might be on that team or not. The Olympic team would add one player then for a total of 12.

Tara VanDerveer was taking a year off from Stanford to coach the U. S. team. The pressure on VanDerveer to produce a winner was palpable. She freely admitted that the 11 players selected by the USA Basketball committee weren't necessarily the 11 she would have picked. In particular, she was bothered by Lobo's inability to create her own shots on offense and McCray's inexperience. She also worried that Edwards and McClain, though proven veterans, were not committed to teamwork.

"I didn't have anything against any of the players personally," VanDerveer said in her book, *Shooting from the Outside*. "But looking at it in May 1995, I felt this wasn't the team that would give us the best chance of winning a gold medal."

On September 26, 1995, as the national team prepared for its 21-game college tour, three California businesspeople announced the formation of a new professional women's league: the American Basketball League. Gary Cavalli, a former sports information director at Stanford; Anne Cribbs, a former U. S. Olympic swimmer, and Steve Hams, a Palo Alto businessman, all were parents of young female basketball players. They found investors among the many computer-based companies in the Silicon Valley. With $20 million for operating expenses, the trio decided the league would own all the teams so that it could control the finances and it handpicked cities that had shown support for women's college basketball: Denver (the Colorado Xplosion); Seattle (Reign); Hartford, Connecticut (New England Blizzard); Columbus, Ohio (Quest); Richmond, Virginia, (Rage); Portland, Oregon

Tara VanDerveer took a timeout from coaching Stanford to coach the 1996 U. S. women's Olympic team.

(Power); Atlanta (Glory), and San Jose, California (Lasers). They enlisted Azzi and other players from the U. S. team to help structure the league. Nine of the 11 national team members attended the press conference and signed contracts to play in the ABL, beginning in October 1996.

A small, Midwestern-based professional league, called the Women's Basketball Association, had been operating successfully since 1993. The WBA had teams in St. Louis, Kansas City, Memphis, Chicago, Nebraska, Oklahoma, Kentucky, and Minnesota. Teams played a 15-game schedule from April through July, with playoffs from mid-July to early August. But the California investors thought the time finally seemed right to take another stab at a nationally based professional league.

The following April, the NBA announced that it too would be starting a new league. Like the WBA, which ceased operation after the 1995 season, the WNBA would play in the summertime. Teams would be based in New York (Liberty), Houston (Comets), Los Angeles (Sparks), Sacramento (Monarchs), Salt Lake City, Utah (Starzz), Cleveland (Rockers), Charlotte, North Carolina (Sting), and Phoenix (Mercury). They would play in NBA arenas and use NBA staff for operations and promotions, beginning in June 1997.

Jennifer Azzi, right, helped create the American Basketball League and promoted it with enthusiasm.

Right away, the competition between the leagues showed the WNBA's superior bargaining power. While ESPN-TV and Nike had shown interest in the ABL, the sports cable network and the biggest corporations sponsoring sports in America decided to sign on with the WNBA. Eight of the nine members of the U. S. team who originally signed with the ABL stuck with it. The average salary in the WNBA was initially about $15,000 as compared to $40,000 in the ABL. The players liked the ABL's higher player salaries, stock options, and traditional winter season.

But Sheryl Swoopes switched leagues, saying she wanted to play for the WNBA team in Texas, her home state. Rebecca Lobo and Lisa Leslie also signed with the WNBA. They liked its ability to promote and market itself through the NBA, and Lobo, Leslie, and Swoopes made much more than the average salary because of their status as premier players. Azzi and Edwards were unhappy with Swoopes for breaking her contract, and the ABL-WNBA debate threatened to fracture the U. S. national team.

"This isn't personal," Swoopes said at the press conference announcing her intention to join the WNBA. "I don't think people should get mad with each other. To me, what this means is there is a lot of interest in women's basketball."

Because of her role on her undefeated Connecticut team just months before, Rebecca Lobo had become the poster girl for women's basketball. She appeared on *Late Night with David Letterman,* had a cameo role in a movie with Tom Cruise, and co-wrote a book with her mother, Ruth Ann, who had battled breast cancer during Rebecca's junior year in college.

Though Lobo was getting star treatment for her past accomplishments, VanDerveer still wasn't convinced that Lobo could help the U. S. team win a gold medal. The former college star found herself sitting on the bench most games, even when the team traveled to Hartford to play her alma mater. But Lobo never complained about playing time, and she tried to deflect the media attention away from herself to Edwards and McClain, the Olympic veterans. "I'm just thrilled to be able to watch these women play, never mind being able to play on the same team," Lobo said. "Some people who've only been fans for the past couple of years may know my name . . . but as they watch our team play, they'll get to know us all."

The U. S. team breezed through its college tour, playing to sellout crowds and winning fans. Little girls wearing $50 team jerseys with Swoopes or Lobo emblazoned on the back, clamored for autographs after every game. One day, as the players drove off after a game in Providence, Rhode Island, they saw a little girl, in tears, chasing the team bus. The players asked the driver to stop so they could give the little girl their autographs. "It didn't take but two minutes to turn the saddest girl in Rhode Island into the happiest," said Swoopes.

The U. S. team didn't lose a game all year—even on a tour of Siberia where the players wore coats and mittens when they weren't playing because the gym was so cold. In China, the U. S. team found itself without Swoopes or McGhee, their leading scorers, because of injuries. Lobo got the chance to show what she could do, scoring 24 and 19 points in two games and boosting her confidence.

When the final Olympic team roster was announced, Lobo found that she had won VanDerveer's confidence, too. The Olympic committee chose Venus Lacey, a 6-foot-4 post player from Louisiana Tech with a reputation for being aggressive on offense and immovable under the basket, as the 12th player.

With a month to go before the Olympics, the U. S. players were feeling burned out. They seemed flat and lifeless in practice. Coach VanDerveer decided to take them on an outdoor, team-building adventure. During the trip, they walked with a partner across cables suspended 30 feet in the air, holding on to each other. VanDerveer paired off with Edwards, the one player she felt she couldn't trust to be a leader. By the time they'd finished the grueling 20-minute course, VanDerveer knew their relationship had changed, "the way you know a shot's going in before it reaches the rim."

The U. S. team's first game at the Atlanta Olympics was against Cuba. The Americans had played and beaten the Cuban team six times in exhibition games in the past year. The U. S. team started slowly but led by 11 at halftime. Every U. S. player got into the game and scored as the United States won, 101–84. The U. S. team ran over its next two opponents, the Ukraine and Zaire, by more than 30 points each, assuring itself a spot in the medal round. Next was undefeated Australia.

In the early-morning hours the day of that game, many players awoke to the sounds of a bomb exploding in Centennial Park, within sight of their hotel. They gathered on the 14th floor in a hallway, then crowded by a window to watch the ambulances arrive and police in riot gear begin their search. The blast killed two people and security was tightened everywhere. But 33,000 fans still crowded into the Georgia Dome to watch the women's game that night.

The Australians, with Michelle Timms at point guard, came out fast and led by six points early in the game. The U. S. team led by three at halftime, but Timms tied the game with a three-pointer early in the second half. Edwards and McClain took over, scoring 44 of the team's 96 points, as the United States won, 96–79.

Lisa Leslie scores for the U. S. team against Australia.

*Nikki McCray slices
around a Brazilian
defender.*

In the quarterfinals, the U. S. players faced Japan, whom they hadn't played since 1994. Japan had surprised everyone by defeating the taller Chinese with three-point shooting and defense. But with Leslie setting a U. S. Olympic record with 35 points, the Americans won, 108–93.

Australia had upset the Russians in an overtime game to set up a rematch with the United States in the semifinals. The Australians weren't prepared for the Americans' switch from a man-to-man defense to a zone. The U. S. team outrebounded Australia, 48–25, and won, 93–71, to advance to the gold-medal game.

The final game was the final event of the 1996 Olympics. That morning, VanDerveer assembled the players in her room to watch one more video. The coach had edited together scenes from every other American gold medal performance. They watched the women's soccer, softball, gymnastics, and synchronized swimming teams earn their gold medals. They realized they were part of something big. A wave that had begun 24 years ago when Title IX had passed was breaking onto the shore as women showed what they could do when given the opportunity. The players laughed and cheered.. When they left for their game, to be played in prime time, they were energized and confident.

Brazil was 7–0, just like the Americans. Brazil's top player, Magic Silva, had sunk five three-pointers in a semifinal win over Ukraine. Another star, Hortencia Oliva, was 36 years old but still as dangerous as when she had scored 32 points against the U. S. team in the 1994 World Championship.

But it was the U. S. shooters who were deadly in the first half, making 72 percent of their shots. VanDerveer took a jittery Leslie out after the first few minutes, but she came back to score 15 points in the half. Silva, meanwhile, was held to a single basket. The U. S. team led by 11 at the half. The Americans continued to dominate in the second half, scoring on 11 of their first 12 possessions. The players stretched the lead to 30 points. Every player scored at least two points. The U. S. team won the game and the gold medal, 111–87. Their point total was the highest ever for a gold-medal game.

The players danced and did cartwheels on the court after the buzzer sounded. They celebrated the culmination of a year of hard work by a team and its coach. The victory was also the culmination of decades of effort by thousands of women to lift the women's basketball game to the level of excellence displayed that day.

"I had always carried in my mind a vision of how basketball should look," wrote VanDerveer in her book. "There should be balance and logic, a little bit of raw genius, some surprise and beauty, and a seamless energy infusing it from beginning to end. This was it."

Into the Spotlight

The gold medal-winning U. S. players celebrate.

12

INTO THE FUTURE

The American Basketball League began its 40-game season on October 18, 1996. Many of the best players in the country, including eight of the 12 members of the 1996 Olympic team, played on the eight ABL teams. Two recent college stars were Jen Rizzotti, the point guard for the University of Connecticut's undefeated 1995 team, and Katie Smith of Ohio State. New England drafted Rizzotti in hopes of drawing her UConn fans to the Blizzard's games. The Columbus Quest, the team nearest Ohio State, drafted Smith. Jackie Joyner-Kersee, the Olympic track star who had played basketball at UCLA, also was drafted to play for Richmond in hopes of attracting publicity and fans.

The remaining roster slots were filled by players chosen from a pool of 570 women who had paid $200 each for a chance to try out the previous summer. More than half had been playing internationally after college. Valerie Still of Columbus was one of them.

Still had played for 12 years in the Italian league after graduating from the University of Kentucky in 1983. In Italy, she led the team to a championship in 1991. Bad fortune befell her in 1992 when she was

Opposite page: Stacey Lovelace defends against Natalie Williams in the 1998 ABL All-Star Game.

nearly killed in a car crash. She broke her hand and nose, fractured two vertebrae, and cracked her pelvis. Doctors said she might never walk again, but she played for two more seasons. Still couldn't resist the chance to play in the ABL, even though in October 1996, she was the league's old lady at 35 and a working mother with a six-month-old son, Aaron.

The ABL averaged 3,500 fans per game its first season, 20 percent higher than the league's projections. The Columbus Quest had the league's lowest attendance, even though it was the league's best team with Smith, Still, and Olympic gold-medalist Nikki McCray. The Quest won the league's first championship in March 1997 by defeating the Richmond Rage, three games to two in a five-game series. Still was named the series MVP, averaging 14 points and eight rebounds per game.

The Quest's attendance problems exemplified the ABL's problems overall. The ABL paid players well, $50,000 to $150,000 a year, and hoped to build fan support through grassroots efforts by players and volunteers rather than through expensive advertising campaigns. The biggest hope was for a television contract from one of the big networks. But by the end of the league's first season, only SportsChannel, which broadcasts games through regional markets, had signed on to televise 24 ABL games. Finding those games was often difficult for fans. Some were played on tape-delay, long after the game was over. As the first season ended, league officials knew they could not sustain the league forever without the attention and sponsors that a major television contract would bring.

By 1997, TV time was not an issue for the NCAA. ESPN-TV had won the contract to broadcast women's college basketball by promising to show a number of collegiate games during the season as well as early-round tournament games leading to the Final Four. The NCAA Final Four had been sold out for months. On the streets, scalpers sold tickets to the semifinal and final games for double or triple their $70 value.

The big story for Tennessee was its all-America sophomore, Chamique Holdsclaw, who had started as a freshman and helped lead the Lady Vols to the 1996 championship. Holdsclaw was a 6-foot-1 forward brought up in Queens, New York, by her grandmother. She led Christ the King High School to four straight state championships.

While the 1996 Lady Vols had won it all, the 1997 team found itself with 10 losses as tournament time approached. The lowest moment of the season was a heartbreaking loss to Old Dominion in January after Tennessee had led by 12 points at the half. But, when the four best teams assembled in Cincinnati in late March, Tennessee was one of them. The two semifinal games on Friday night featured Tennessee against Notre Dame and Stanford against Old Dominion.

Heavily favored Stanford had all-American Kate Starbird, point guard Jamila Wideman, and recently recruited volleyball player Kristin Folkl to lead them. The first half was all Kate Starbird as she banked incredibly long three-pointers off the backboard glass. Stanford led at the half, 37–30. Old Dominion shut down Starbird in the second half, and, with seconds to play, ODU tied the score and sent the game into overtime. Old Dominion's Ticha Penicheiro was the hero in overtime, stealing the ball and making a crucial free throw to give ODU the thrilling victory, 83–82.

The 1997 NCAA semifinal between Old Dominion and Stanford featured more drama than most fans could stand.

In the other semifinal, Tennessee started off slowly and only led by one at halftime. But three straight steals to begin the second half put the Vols ahead of Notre Dame, 33–28. Every time Notre Dame's all-American Beth Morgan sank a three-pointer or layup, Holdsclaw answered with a three-pointer or layup of her own. Tennessee finally pulled away with six minutes to go and wound up winning, 80–66. Holdsclaw led all scorers with 31 points. "Without her, we'd be on spring break," said Coach Summitt of Holdsclaw. "I think she's going to be one of the greatest to ever have played the game."

ESPN televised the final game, on Easter Sunday evening. The game was surrounded, it seemed, by

*Chamique Holdsclaw led
Tennessee to a thrilling
comeback.*

pioneers of women's basketball. The officials in-
cluded Dee Kanter and Violet Palmer, the first two
women to ever referee in the National Basketball
Association. The broadcast booth featured Ann
Meyers analyzing the action, Nancy Lieberman-
Cline doing sideline interviews, and former players
Rebecca Lobo, Robin Roberts, and Mimi Griffin
doing halftime analysis and interviews.

Even the two coaches, Summitt and ODU's
Wendy Larry, were pioneers. Larry played for the
Lady Monarchs in the mid-1970s and was an assistant coach during ODU's national championship
years in the early 1980s. After a long slide out of the
top echelon of teams, Larry had guided Old
Dominion back into contention.

Summitt had been coaching at Tennessee for close
to 20 years and earned more than the men's basketball coach there. During a press conference before
the semifinals, Summitt acknowledged that she
had been approached about coaching men. "I don't
consider it a step up," said Summitt. "I really love
the women's game."

As Summitt's team headed to the arena for the
final game Sunday night, she showed them a video-
tape of the last few minutes of their loss to Old
Dominion in January. The players silently vowed to
win this time.

At game time, a sea of orange filled the arena with
deafening cheers as the school band played the
Tennessee fight song, "Rocky Top." Summitt's game
plan to keep Penicheiro from penetrating into the
middle of the key worked well in the first half. The
Lady Vols led by 12 at the break. But ODU took the
momentum in the second half. Key steals by
Penicheiro and clutch three-pointers from Aubrey
Ember and Amber Eller pulled ODU ahead by two
with seven minutes to play.

Then Holdsclaw took over. She scored four baskets in succession, grabbed a big rebound, blocked a
shot, and fed a teammate for another basket to put
Tennessee up by six. She scored two more points on
free throws as the game wound down. When the
buzzer sounded, Tennessee had won its second

Tennessee coach Pat Head Summitt and her son, Tyler, whoop it up.

straight national championship, 68–59. Holdsclaw won MVP honors for her 24 points in the title game.

Summitt and her six-year-old son, Tyler, beamed as they cut the cords from the net during the on-court victory celebration. "Fifth in the Southeastern Conference and first in the country," said Summitt as she summed up her team's accomplishments after the championship game. "Ten years from now, this season will stand out because of what we had to overcome."

With the NCAA tournament over, the question became: which league would the talented senior class of basketball players choose? The ABL seemed to win the bidding war. Kara Wolters of Connecticut, Beth Morgan and Katryna Gaither of Notre Dame, and Kate Starbird of Stanford all signed with the ABL.

But the WNBA's promotional campaign, which began in May 1997, proved the power of marketing. The catchy slogan, "We've got next," and slick commercials featuring Lobo and Leslie piqued the curiosity of national reporters who had ignored the ABL. Junior high and high school girls tacked up the

The WNBA lured Nancy
Lieberman-Cline back
onto the court.

free WNBA posters that league officials gave away at summer camps.

Oldtimers such as Nancy Lieberman-Cline, Cheryl Miller, Lynette Woodard, and Nancy Darsch knew a good opportunity when they saw it. They all wished the ABL well but. . . . Woodard gave up her job as a stockbroker to play for the WNBA's Cleveland franchise. Miller signed on to coach the Phoenix Mercury. Darsch, who had just been fired after 12 years at Ohio State, chose to coach the New York Liberty instead of the ABL's New England Blizzard. Lieberman-Cline put down her microphone for ESPN to pick up a basketball again, for the Phoenix Mercury of the WNBA.

Lieberman-Cline said the WNBA, with its summer schedule, made sense for personal and business reasons. She could continue to broadcast college games and have more time with her husband and two-year-old son, T. J. "You'd have to think economically, business-wise, that the WNBA will be here for a long time," said Lieberman-Cline.

The WNBA's nationally televised debut on June 21, 1997, ended up being panned by the national media. The WNBA players had only practiced together for three weeks before opening day. News articles and broadcasts focused on the sloppy play and Leslie's missed dunk early in the action. But the 14,284 fans at the Los Angeles Forum—the largest crowd ever to watch a women's pro game—couldn't have cared less about the quality of play or the outcome. "They were even cheering for free throws," said Leslie, who finished with 16 points and 14 rebounds as Los Angeles defeated New York, 67–57. "We were overwhelmed by it."

In New York, the Liberty jumped onto the front page of *The New York Times* and was featured in *Sports Illustrated* because of the tremendous fan support. Sportswriters marveled at the vast numbers of families with small children, whole basketball teams of teenage girls, elderly women, and lesbian couples sitting side by side in the $8 to $45 seats at Liberty games in Madison Square Garden. The Liberty drew close to 12,000 in the first half of the season. After games, many players spent an hour or two signing autographs. They chatted with the fans, kissed their cheeks, posed for photos with them, and thanked them for coming to the game or buying their jersey. Teresa Weatherspoon of the Liberty had played her college career for Louisiana Tech in relative obscurity. She loved being a star. "If my being here makes their day, it makes my day," said Weatherspoon to a *New York Times* reporter as she signed autographs and high-fived her fans after a Liberty game.

By the end of the WNBA's 24-game season, the league had doubled its attendance projections, drawing an average of 9,000 fans a game. The league's one-game semifinals and the final game between the Houston Comets and the New York Liberty were sellouts. And the final game garnered a 2.9 TV rating even though it aired opposite U. S. Open tennis and college football games.

Teresa Weatherspoon signs a jersey for an eager fan.

Houston defeated the Liberty, 65–51, in a one-game championship to win the first WNBA title. The MVP of the series and the season was Houston's shooting guard, Cynthia Cooper, the former USC star. Many fans had cheered for her during the season when she played while shuttling her mother to chemotherapy treatments for breast cancer.

The WNBA's success lured Nikki McCray away from the ABL's Columbus Quest in the fall of 1997. Losing McCray was a major blow to the ABL as it prepared for its second season. Still, the ABL re-signed 52 of its 54 free agents that fall, including Katie Smith, who had been courted by the WNBA. The Richmond franchise moved to Philadelphia and the league added a team in Long Beach, California. But the ABL still was showing only 24 games a year on Fox Sports Network. Without a major television contract, the league was having a difficult time getting sponsors other than Reebok.

The ABL's second season featured an all-star game at Disney World in Orlando. The weekend featured a slam-dunk contest, but while Lisa Leslie's missed dunk was big news when the WNBA began, many reporters ignored Sylvia Crawley's winning

*Sylvia Crawley's
blindfolded dunk*

blindfolded dunk. Crawley, of Portland, took two long, graceful strides and then laid the ball up over the rim with her eyes covered. Other participants in the contest jumped up and down and screamed right along with the fans.

Columbus again won the league championship, despite the absence of McCray. The Quest lost the first two games to Long Beach and had to win three in a row to capture the crown. Valerie Still again was named the series MVP after she led the Quest with 25 points in the final game, an 86–81 thriller.

"Yeah, I'm old, but after all I've been through to get here it's a pride thing now," she told reporters after the game. "No way can I back down. This is about a movement, almost a kind of civil rights movement to show people women can be tough and talented and play basketball at a high level."

Not many people witnessed how tough Still was. Battelle Hall in Columbus was sold out, with 6,313 people on hand, but the game wasn't seen live on television in either Columbus or Long Beach because of local programming conflicts. The Quest's series also had to compete with the first two rounds of NCAA basketball playoffs for women and men.

The 1998 NCAA women's playoffs again featured Tennessee defending its national title as well as hoping to become the first women's team to win three championships in a row. Tennessee's challenger was an old nemesis, Louisiana Tech, which was making its ninth trip to the NCAA Final Four. Barmore's Lady Techsters defeated Kay Yow's North Carolina State team in the semifinals. Tennessee defeated Arkansas, which was making its first Final Four appearance. The Lady Vols brought a 38–0 record into the title game in Kansas City.

Pat Summitt had four of the previous year's top high school seniors: Semeka Randall, Tamicka Catchings, Teresa Geter, and Kristen Clement. Catchings led all scorers with 27 points but Holdsclaw carried the team, scoring 16 of her 25 points in the first half, as the Lady Vols easily defeated Louisiana Tech, 93–75, to earn their third title in a row.

"If you look at the Final Four, this is it, this is our Super Bowl," Summitt said. The Lady Vols earned congratulations from the White House, but their trip to Michael Jordan's office in Chicago was just as thrilling, especially for Holdsclaw. She hadn't expected Jordan to know who she was. When he not only called her by name but also challenged her to a game of one-on-one, she was speechless.

Once the college season ended, the WNBA announced that it had signed 9 of the top 15 college players, including seven Kodak All-Americans. The

A History of Basketball for Girls and Women

Cynthia Cooper won the first three MVP trophies the WNBA awarded.

WNBA also added teams in Washington, D. C., and Detroit for the 1998 season. Nancy Lieberman-Cline retired from playing to coach the Detroit Shock, and Nikki McCray was assigned to the Washington Mystics.

The league's average attendance soared past 10,000 for the 1998 season. The Houston Comets, led again by Cynthia Cooper, defeated the Phoenix Mercury, 80–71, to win the championship. Sheryl Swoopes, back from maternity leave, had 16 points. The league then announced two more expansion teams for 1999, in Orlando and Minnesota. Another two teams, Miami and Indianapolis, would be added in 2000, toward the goal of WNBA teams in all 29 NBA cities.

Meanwhile, the ABL prepared for its third season. Attendance at ABL games in the second season had increased 23 percent to an average of 4,300 per game. The league replaced two struggling franchises— Atlanta and Long Beach—with teams in Nashville and Chicago. The league also announced that CBS-TV would be broadcasting two championship series games in 1998–99.

But potential sponsors still weren't convinced that the TV deal at the end of the season would generate enough exposure to warrant investing heavily in the league at the beginning of the season. As the first games approached, some of the ABL's staunchest supporters decided to move on. Quest coach Brian Agler left Columbus when the WNBA offered him a coaching position. Dawn Staley finally decided it was time to join her friend Leslie in the WNBA.

Cavalli announced plans to increase the ABL's advertising budget, hoping to capitalize on the fact that the NBA was not playing because of labor problems, but the advertising campaign did not produce the results that the ABL needed. Two months into the season, poor attendance and nervous creditors forced the league to declare bankruptcy on December 22, 1998. According to court records, the league was $10 million in debt with only $500,000 in assets. "I do think people shied away from competing with the NBA," player agent Andy Brandt told *The San Jose Mercury News.* "Sponsors and networks want to be with the cachet of the NBA."

The abrupt end shocked players and fans in Hartford, San Jose, and Seattle, where attendance was among the league's best. Players on other teams weren't surprised. They had seen sparse crowds of fewer than 1,000 fans in some cities. As the players headed home, many hoped to catch on with the WNBA but mourned the loss of what they considered a league of their own.

San Jose didn't completely lack women's basketball in 1999, thanks to the NCAA women's Final Four. Tennessee and Chamique Holdsclaw would try for an unprecedented fourth championship in a row, and all the analysts predicted they would succeed. But Holdsclaw and Kellie Jolly, Tennessee's two seniors, played the worst games of their careers in the regional final. Duke University stunned the Lady Vols, 69–63, in Greensboro, North Carolina.

With Tennessee out of the running, Duke, Georgia, Louisiana Tech, and Purdue each felt they had a shot at the national title. Duke had 6-foot-5 center Michele VanGorp, a skinny blond senior with a stunning hook shot as well as a smooth three-pointer. VanGorp and another Duke player had transferred from Purdue after the coach who recruited them, Lin Dunn, was fired during their freshman year. Georgia was led by identical twins Kelly and Coco Miller, from Rochester, Minnesota. In the semifinals, Duke easily defeated Georgia.

Purdue's three-guard offense, led by best friends Stephanie White-McCarty and Ukari Figgs, withstood a late-game run by Louisiana Tech to make it to the final. Many doubted that Purdue, without a dominant center, could match up against VanGorp. The first half of the championship game seemed to prove that. Purdue shot 29 percent from two-point range and was 0-for-6 in three-pointers. Duke led 22–17 in one of the lowest-scoring halves in NCAA history.

Figgs, held scoreless in the first half, took charge in the second, bringing Purdue back into the lead with 13 minutes to play. Purdue's lead increased to

Guard Ukari Figgs led Purdue to the 1999 NCAA Championship.

A History of Basketball for Girls and Women

five with four minutes to go. But then White-McCarty, known as much for her stable presence as her passing and shooting, twisted her ankle. As White-McCarty pleaded with the trainer to wrap the ankle, Figgs assured her the team would win the game for her. Duke failed to score another basket in the last four minutes. Purdue won, 62–45, and was the first team from the Big Ten Conference to win the NCAA title. Figgs, who scored 18 points in the second half, was named the tournament's Most Valuable Player.

Although Holdsclaw had lost the last game of her season for the first time in her life, she was the first player drafted by the WNBA. Many veterans of the defunct ABL were also first-round picks in 1999. The Houston Comets won their third WNBA championship in a row, defeating the New York Liberty. Comet players dedicated the title to Kim Perrot, a teammate who died of cancer during the season.

Women's basketball finally had enough talent to sustain a professional league and fuel college dynasties, like Tennessee, and challengers, like Duke and Purdue. And more talent was on the way. A 1998 study showed that one-fifth of the 2.4 million girls playing high school sports in the United States played basketball. Women's basketball at smaller colleges in Divisions II and III also grew tremendously, giving thousands more girls a chance to play after high school.

Four girls enjoy a friendly game of basketball.

Girls have, finally, won the chance to play basketball any way they want. They can play intensely all year round or once a week in a recreational league. They can devote all their free time to practice and weight training, or they can play in friendly pick-up games when the mood strikes. But, as members of the 1996 Olympic team showed with their spontaneous cartwheels after their gold-medal victory, girls at all levels can't help but play the game of basketball with what Senda Berenson once described as "enthusiasm and delight."

Further Reading

Two books—*Coming on Strong, Gender and Sexuality in Twentieth-Century Women's Sports* by Susan K. Cahn (The Free Press, 1994) and *A Century of Women's Basketball, From Frailty to Final Four*, a collection of articles edited by Joan S. Hult and Marianna Trekell (American Alliance for Health, Physical Education and Recreation, 1991)—were invaluable to me as I gathered information on the rich history of girls basketball. Though both books were written by college professors, they are reasonably accessible to the average reader and are loaded with insights and information, particularly on the first half of the century.

The Amazing Basketball Book, The First 100 Years by Bob Hill and Randall Baron (Devyn Press, 1988) about the early evolution of the rules of the game was also helpful and fun to read.

Three books about Babe Didrikson shed light on her basketball career and basketball in general in the 1930s. They are: *Whatta Gal, the Babe Didrikson Story* by William Oscar Johnson and Nancy P. Williamson (Little, Brown, 1977); *Babe, The Life and Legend of Babe Didrikson Zaharias* by Susan Cayleff (University of Illinois Press, 1995); and Didrikson's autobiography, *This Life I've Led* (Buccaneer Books, 1994).

For insights on basketball in Iowa, I am grateful to E. Wayne Cooley, who still heads the Iowa Girls High School Athletic Union and never tires of talking about girls basketball. Cooley helped me contact several players and townspeople who experienced the hysteria of tournament time in Iowa. He also provided me with two helpful books: *Only In Iowa* by Jim Enright (Iowa Girls' High School Athletic Association, 1976) and *From Six on Six to Full-Court Press, A Century of Iowa Girls' Basketball* by Janice A. Beran (Iowa State University Press, 1993).

For information on Maine's basketball history, I am grateful to retired *Portland Press Herald* sportswriter Dick Doyle, Deering High School graduate

Basketball's founding mother—Senda Berenson

Arthur Peterson, ex-player and coach Stella Waterman McLean of Farmington, who shared her scrapbook and some great memories, and the Westbrook Historical Society.

For information on AAU basketball, I relied on interviews with two great ladies, Eunies Futch and Eckie Jordan, who played for Hanes Hosiery in the 1950s. I also am grateful to Elva Bishop, who sent me a copy of her 1997 documentary film for North Carolina Public Television called "Women's Basketball: The Road to Respect." Though the Women's Basketball Hall of Fame in Knoxville was not yet open when I was doing my research, Valerie Key, their chief researcher, helped me find Bishop and other early-era players. The Hall opened in June of 1999.

The Naismith Memorial Basketball Hall of Fame in Springfield, Massachusetts, also proved to be a good source of information. Thanks to the people there for setting up my interview with Cheryl Miller when she was inducted into the Hall of Fame in 1995.

For early collegiate and Olympic history, I relied on selections from several encyclopedia-like books: *Nike is a Goddess, The History of Women in Sports* (Grove/Atlantic, Inc., 1998); *The Women's Sports Encyclopedia* by Robert Markel (Henry Holt and Company, Inc., 1997); *Great Women in Sports* by Anne Janette Johnson (Visible Ink Press, 1996), and *At the Rim, A Celebration of Women's Collegiate Basketball* (Thomasson-Grant, Inc., 1991). While *At the Rim* is a coffee-table book of photographs, the introduction by Patsy Neal, who played on the Flying Hutchersons and went to several world championship tournaments, was invaluable about the 1950s and 1960s.

Tara VanDerveer's autobiography, *Shooting from the Outside* (Avon Books, 1998), was mainly about the 1996 Olympic basketball team, but it also included some great personal insights and lots of details about the early years of intercollegiate women's basketball. If I could only read one book about women's basketball, I might choose VanDerveer's.

As I approached the 1970s, '80s, and '90s, I relied more often on magazine articles and personal interviews. Most of the research for the chapter on the failed WBL of the early 1980s came from interviews I did with players, coaches, and league officials while writing about the demise of the league for newspaper and magazine articles in 1980 and 1981. I attended the 1997 NCAA Final Four in Cincinnati and several WNBA games in 1998 to interview such coaches as Nancy Lieberman-Cline, Marianne Stanley, Pat Head Summitt, and Tara VanDerveer and players such as Chamique Holdsclaw, Ticha Penicheiro, Rebecca Lobo, Lynette Woodard, and Kellie Jolly.

Four books that gave me lots of insight into modern Olympic and professional women basketball players were: *Shooting Stars, The Women of Pro Basketball* by Bill Gutman (Random House, Inc., 1998), *Playing in a New League* by Sara Gogol (NTC Publishing Group, 1998); *The Best of the Best in Basketball* by Rachel Rutledge (Millbrook Press, 1998), and *Venus to the Hoop* by Sara Corbett (Bantam Doubleday Dell Publishing Group, 1997).

As the century came to a close, many more autobiographies and biographies of female basketball players and coaches were finding their way into print. *Reach for the Summitt* (Broadway Books, 1998), Pat Head Summitt's book about her coaching philosophy, is full of highlights from the 1997 season. *Raise the Roof* by Summitt (Broadway Books, 1999) is devoted to the championship season of 1998. *She Got Game* by Cynthia Cooper (Time Warner, 1999) sheds light on what it was like to play in Cheryl Miller's shadow in college, in Europe, and on the WNBA's most successful team in its first three years. *In These Girls, Hope is a Muscle* (Warner Books, Inc., 1995) is the fascinating chronicle of one high school basketball season, made more interesting by the fact that the star of the team was Jamila Wideman, who played at Stanford and in the WNBA.

Index

Photo and Illustration Acknowledgments

The images in this book are used with the permission of: Norm Perdue/NBA Photos, p. 2; Corbis/Bettmann, pp. 6, 8, 14, 16, 21, 31, 44, 98, 138; Brown Brothers, pp. 10, 22, 28, 29, 32, 33, 34, 36, 41, 48, 50; Smith College Archives/Smith College, pp. 11, 13, 15, 26, 27, 62, 139; Library of Congress, pp. 18, 40; Photos Courtesy State Historical Society of Iowa-Iowa City, pp. 37, 52, 55, 56, 57; Runyon Photograph Collection, Center for American History, University of Texas at Austin, pp. 38 (E/VN09747), 42 (E/VN03731); Babe Didrikson Zaharias Collection, John Gray Library, Lamar University, p. 47; Corbis/Bettmann-UPI, pp. 49, 72, 74, 85, 86, 88, 89, 90, 92, 93, 95, 103, 104, 106, 108; Courtesy Arkansas History Commission, pp. 51, 71; Stella Waterman, pp. 58, 59; Lambert/Archive Photos, p. 64; AP/Wide World Photos, pp. 68, 76, 113, 125; Wayland Baptist University, p. 69; Archive Photos/Gerald Davis, p. 77; California State University-Fullerton Athletics, p. 78; Courtesy Indiana University Athletic Department, p. 79; Courtesy of the Robert Halvey Collection of the Philadelphia Archdiocesan Archives, p. 81; Iowa Girls' High School Athletic Union, p. 102; © ALLSPORT USA/Mike Powell, pp. 105, 112; © ALLSPORT USA/Tony Duffy, p. 110; SportsChrome East/West, pp. 111, 124; © ALLSPORT USA/Jim Gund, pp. 114, 115; © ALLSPORT USA/Otto Greule, p. 116; © ALLSPORT USA/Jonathan Daniel, pp. 117, 129, 130; Noren Trotman/NBA Photos, 118; Joanne Lannin, p. 119; © ALLSPORT USA/Andy Lyons, pp. 120, 134; Nathaniel S. Butler/NBA Photos, p. 121; R. Eckert/NBA Photos, p. 123; © ALLSPORT USA/Peter Traylor, 126; © ALLSPORT USA/Michelle S. Brady, p. 132; Jennifer Pottheiser/NBA Photos, p. 133; Bill Baptist/NBA Photos, p. 136; Purdue University, p. 137.

Front cover, right, Sam Forenich/NBA Photos; back to front cover, Brown Brothers; back cover, Nathaniel S. Butler/WNBA Photos.